ADRIANA ANGEL was born in Colombia in 1955. She studied Communicative Arts at the University of the District of Columbia, Washington DC, before going to Nicaragua in 1980, where she worked in television and established the photography department and trained workers in the Nicaraguan women's organisation, AMNLAE. She has contributed photographs on the theme of Nicaraguan women to numerous publications and exhibitions both in Nicaragua and abroad, and has worked extensively as a freelance photographer in television and films. She co-directed 'The Eye of the Mask', a Canadian film production on popular culture in Nicaragua.

FIONA MACINTOSH was born in Edinburgh in 1951 and first went to Nicaragua in 1981. From then until 1984 she worked mainly as a graphic designer on numerous publications, posters and exhibitions, including one on the history of ANMLAE. As writer, designer and photographer she has produced various English/Spanish publications and in 1984 established a publication design department for the Nicaraguan Union of Rural Workers (ATC). Recently, in collaboration with Four Corners Film Co-operative, London, she has produced a film based on material in *The Tiger's Milk*, and she is now co-producing a film in Nicaragua.

THE TIGER'S MILK
WOMEN OF NICARAGUA

Adriana Angel
Fiona Macintosh

SEAVER BOOKS

Henry Holt and Company

New York

The cover photograph was taken during the 1985 ceasefire in North Zelaya in the Atlantic Coast region, when thousands of war-displaced families like this Miskito mother and her children were able to return to their river communities near to the Honduran border. Since then renewed counter-revolutionary action has again displaced most of these families.

Published in the United States by Seaver Books/Henry Holt and Company, Inc., 521 Fifth Avenue, New York, New York 10175.

Library of Congress Catalog Card Number: 87-60789

ISBN: 0-8050-0638-9

First American Edition

Designer: Fiona Macintosh

Printed in Great Britain by Jolly & Barber Ltd, Rugby

10 9 8 7 6 5 4 3 2 1

ISBN 0-8050-0638-9

Contents

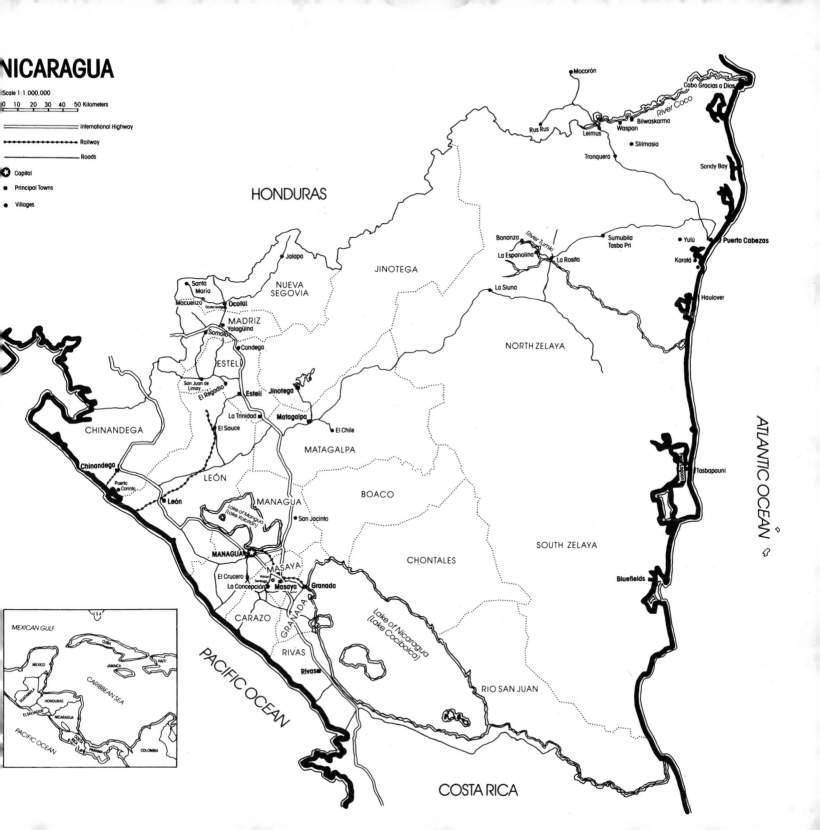

NICARAGUA

Scale 1:1.000.000

0 10 20 30 40 50 Kilometers

————————— International Highway
•••••••••••• Railway
————————— Roads

✪ Capital
■ Principal Towns
• Villages

HONDURAS

Mocorón

Cabo Gracias a Dios

River Coco

Rus Rus
Leimus
Waspan
Bilwaskarma
Siilmasia

Tronquera

Sandy Bay

Jalapa

JINOTEGA

Bonanza
River Tumki
Sumubila
Tasba Pri
Yulú
Puerto Cabezas

La Espanolina
La Rosita
Karatá

Santa
Maria

NUEVA
SEGOVIA

La Siuna

Haulover

Macuelizo   Ocotal
MADRIZ   Ocotal bridge
Yalaguina
Somoto
Condega

NORTH ZELAYA

ESTELÍ

San Juan de
Limay
El Regadío   Estelí   Jinotega
La Trinidad   Matagalpa
El Sauce   El Chile

CHINANDEGA

MATAGALPA

Tasbapauni

Chinandega
Puerto Corinto
León

LEÓN

MANAGUA

BOACO

SOUTH ZELAYA

Lake of Managua
(Lake Xolotlán)
San Jacinto

CHONTALES

MANAGUA
MASAYA
El Crucero
La Concepción   Masaya   Granada

Volcán
Santiago

Bluefields

CARAZO

GRANADA

RIVAS

Lake of Nicaragua
(Lake Cocibolca)

Rivas

RIO SAN JUAN

ATLANTIC OCEAN

PACIFIC OCEAN

COSTA RICA

MEXICAN GULF

U.S.A.

MEXICO
CUBA
HAITI
JAMAICA

CARIBBEAN SEA

GUATEMALA
HONDURAS
ELSALVADOR
NICARAGUA
COSTA RICA
PANAMA
COLOMBIA

PACIFIC OCEAN

Abbreviations

AMNLAE   Asociación de Mujeres Nicaragüenses 'Luisa Amanda Espinoza'
Association of Nicaraguan Women, 'Luisa Amanda Espinoza'

ALPROMISU   Alianza para el Desarrollo Miskito y Sumu
Alliance for Miskito and Sumu Development

ARDE   Alianza Revolucionario Democrática
Democratic Revolutionary Alliance

ATC   Asociación de Trabajadores del Campo
Rural Workers' Association

CDS   Comíté de Defensa Sandinista
Sandinista Defence Committee

CIA   Central Intelligence Agency

CST   Central Sandinista de Trabajadores
Sandinista Workers' Federation

FDN   Fuerza Democrática Nicaraguense
Nicaraguan Democratic Force

FSLN   Frente Sandinista de Liberación Nacional
Sandinista National Liberation Front

MISURA   Miskito, Sumu, Rama

MISURASATA   Miskito, Sumu, Rama, Sandinista, Asla Takanka
Miskito, Sumu, Rama, All Together

Introduction

Miriam Suarez had been longing for a baby. When the Sandinistas ended Somoza's long dictatorship in 1979, many of her friends had celebrated a new-found faith in the future by having children. She and her husband had been trying for a child without success for six years, and there was great joy when at last Miriam found that she was pregnant.

The next few months were tiring, for Miriam went on working long hours, but she felt exhilarated. During the last month, however, she began to grow uneasy; for several days she did not feel the baby move. Her gynaecologist had abandoned Nicaragua for the comforts of Miami, but another doctor assured her that all was well. He was wrong. The placenta had ceased to function, and a few days later Miriam was rushed to hospital for an emergency Caesarian. There was no anaesthetic for the operation, as stocks had run out, but the baby was born alive.

The next day, lying alone in the overcrowded ward, a nurse came to tell Miriam that the little girl was dead. The incubator had broken down; it was made in the US and there were no spare parts available. Soon after she returned home, Miriam's temperature soared. A bad internal infection had set in, but because of the shortage of foreign exchange in the country the drugs she needed could not be obtained. Her recovery was slow and painful, and now she never speaks of her experience.

Who is Miriam Suarez? A market woman living in a *barrio*, a poor neighbourhood of some provincial town? A *campesina*, or peasant woman, from a remote rural region? She is a senior official in a government ministry who attended the main women's hospital in the capital, Managua: a hospital which is part of a health system whose priority is maternal and child care.

This is the reality of living in a poor country whose attempts to build a better future are blocked by economic sanctions, internal destabilisation provoked from outside, and the effects of a counter-revolutionary (Contra) war promoted by the United States. In the west, whatever our complaints about inadequate state health care, there are certain basic facilities we take for granted: the availability of professional consultation, intensive-care units for our children, provision of drugs and anaesthetics. In Nicaragua, none of these things can be assumed.

This is the context within which not only the achievements of the Sandinistas but also the aims of the revolution and of different sectors within it must be set. The Nicaraguan women's struggle takes place in conditions very different from our own. Their testimonies should help us to understand it on its own terms, and not in the light of preconceptions. For them, women's emancipation is rooted in the fight for their country's freedom. When they speak out in this book, they tell not only of their particular oppression and specific gains, but also of a national history, a past which lives with them and shapes both their existence and the way they see the world.

Throughout this history, and the women's accounts of it, runs a common theme: Nicaragua's vicious circle of poverty and North American aggression. Unless freed from the treadmill of basic survival, women cannot move forward; if the revolution is destroyed, the advances they have made will be erased. This is the reality from which they speak.

Nicaragua and North American Control

The official history of Nicaragua as taught in Somoza's schools dwelt on the civilising influence first of Spain and then of the United States. The real story, one of foreign control and popular resistance, was suppressed. Now, the way in which those in this book recall their history reflects the Sandinista project of recovering the people's past and of forging a new sense of national identity denied by foreign domination.

When the Spanish settled in the populous Pacific plains of Nicaragua in 1523, their initial enterprise was to export more than one million Indians as slave labour to the gold mines of Peru. The Indian population of the remote Atlantic region fared better, as the Spanish did not settle in the area. Their history then followed a distinct and complex course to which I shall return later. But on the Pacific side, the original inhabitants who remained were decimated by war, forced labour and disease, and today only a few small indigenous communities, such as that of Rita López (q.v.), still remain. The majority of Nicaragua's total population of three million is Mestizo, mainly of mixed Indian and Spanish ancestry.

On independence from Spain in 1821, Nicaragua exchanged Spanish for North American control. This was exercised both by overt intervention and by indirect influence through supporting suitable presidential candidates and manipulating party rivalries. Ironically, in terms of contemporary connotations, the Liberal Party became the power base of the Somoza dynasty from the 1930s onwards, with the Conservatives in opposition. But at the end of the nineteenth century it was a Liberal president, Zelaya, who attempted to establish a modern nation state. Conflicting with US interests, Zelaya was overthrown in 1909 by the Marines, who remained in direct occupation. Popular resistance, such as that of Benjamin Zeledon in 1912, was crushed, and the rebels massacred.

Zeledon's funeral procession, it is said, filed past the small house of the youth named Augusto César Sandino. Fifteen years later, in 1927, Sandino led his own guerrilla army of workers and *campesinos* against the Marines. Fiercely nationalistic and anti-imperialist, he also opposed corrupt ruling-class control, and his peasant literacy classes and agricultural co-operatives were part of a plan to transfer political and economic power to the people. Sandino succeeded in ousting the Marines, who withdrew in 1933, but the following year, as he left the palace after talks with President Sacasa, he was ambushed in the night and shot. His followers were executed, the co-operatives destroyed and his name expunged from official history.

The annihilation of Sandino was arranged, with the blessing of the US Minister in Managua, by General Anastasio Somoza Garcia, head of the National Guard which replaced the Marines. Assuming the presidency, Somoza took control of Nicaragua as Washington's stooge. He was executed in 1956 by a poet, Rigoberto López, but was succeeded by his son, then by the latter's brother, Anastasio Somoza Debayle, who continued the regime. Abandoning the Atlantic Coast to neglect and US commerce, Somoza ran the Pacific as his private fief. The National Guard, acting as a personal army, maintained the economic and political stranglehold of Somoza's circle, until broken in 1979 by Sandino's own successor, the Sandinista National Liberation Front (FSLN).

Economy, Poverty and Women's Oppression

In return for his hegemony, Somoza sold the Nicaraguan economy to the United States. This was not so much a matter of direct exploitation of resources – there was substantial US investment in the Atlantic Coast area, but little in the Pacific region – but the export crops which came to dominate the economy, the cotton, coffee, tobacco, sugar and beef, served mainly to satisfy US demand. The small farms of rice, maize and beans for the home market received few resources, and as the large estates devoured land and labour *campesinos* were driven from their property. Some moved to remoter regions, some lost all their land and depended on the pittance of rural wages. Others rented small plots from large landowners for cash or labour, or in exchange for part of their harvest. From the owner's point of view, as expounded by the rancher and sugar farmer Briones (q.v.), this system of sharecropping seemed suitably paternalistic, part of a protective feudal relationship between employer and employee. But for their workers, such as Otilia Casco Cruz's family (*q.v.*), to mortgage part of your produce in advance meant pawning your security, solvency and freedom. By the end of Somoza's regime, only a minority of *campesino* families owned enough land to support themselves, and the demands of export crops created a peasantry partly dependent on waged labour and a pattern of seasonal labour at harvest time which still exists today. This temporary workforce comes from town and country. Often whole families set off, with women and children crowded on to the lorries which rumble up the rocky tracks to the northern coffee plantations. Half the pickers in the hot dusty cotton fields along the Pacific Coast are women.

In many families, the women's earnings are essential. At least half of all Nicaraguan households are headed by women, and in Managua the number is even higher. Men come and go, but do not necessarily support the children they leave behind. This is not just because of *machismo*, the flamboyant form of sexism displayed by men and internalised by women throughout Latin America. Attitudes have deeper roots; instability is built into society. Workers often earn too little to support a family, and seasonal labour and the search for jobs leads to liaisons, not to permanent relationships. In the past, robbed of land, respect and political expression, men took out their frustration on their women or numbed themselves with drink. Old habits die hard, and violence and alcoholism do not make for stable homes.

Struggling to maintain their families, women bore the brunt of the poverty engendered by Somoza's regime; health and education facilities were scarce and in the isolated countryside almost non-existent. Seventy per cent of Nicaraguans suffered some degree of malnutrition, with even more living below the breadline. Ninety per cent of the rural population had no latrines, let alone running water, and disease was rife.

In these conditions, children were always at risk. The official figure for infant mortality under Somoza was 12 per cent but *campesinas* like Rita López and her mother (*q.v.*) could lose half their children, a cruel reality when in Nicaragua children are so deeply loved and treasured. Women were constantly pregnant owing to lack of contraception and because frequent miscarriage from illness or overwork, combined with infant mortality, meant that a woman needed several births to ensure that she had children who might survive to adulthood. Young children, too, helped to maintain their parents by working in the fields or selling on street corners, and it was a woman's sons, rather than her husband, who supported her in old age. She in turn would care for her grandchildren while her daughter went out to work.

Both the ideology of *machismo* and the Catholic Church held that women's place was in the home. But long before the present women's association was urging women to enter production, nearly half of the female population over ten were earning a living, and most mothers had to work outside the home. Jobs were scarce. The emphasis on agro-exports had limited the development of industry, and although 17 per cent of women workers were in manufacturing this included independent artisans. Nearly 25 per cent of Nicaraguan women worked for themselves as street and market sellers of fruit, vegetables, cooked food, cold drinks, cosmetics, clothes and crockery. Now, with the revolution, women feel more free to leave the rigid routine of poorly paid employment and set up their own stalls or handcarts. One of the most familiar sights on Nicaraguan streets is the *vendedora*, her frilly apron stretched across her stomach to hold the cash. In contrast, another common solution for survival, prostitution, is now reduced. Declining too is the largest category of all women's employment under Somoza, the army of *empleadas*, the exploited domestic servants found in every middle-class home. Helena Williams, Lesbia Joya Diaz, Adela Cruz, Carmen López and María Borjas (*q.v.*) all did their stint as cooks, cleaners, child-minders or maids, and most remember the experience with bitterness.

The drudgery of women's lives emerges clearly in the recollections of childhood, youth and mothers' lives included in this book. Poverty compounded by *machismo* meant hunger, exhaustion, insecurity and worry. Yet not for all did motherhood mean sacrifice and resignation, as it did for Lesbia Joya Diaz (*q.v.*); for some to be a mother meant to fight with determination and ingenuity to fend for the family. Hard experience outside the home was coupled with the capacity to take risks and enter into conflict, and it was this resourcefulness of Nicaraguan women which became part of the Sandinista strength.

The Sandinista National Liberation Front

Despite suppression, Sandino's memory survived as a symbol of national resistance, and in 1961 took on a new life in the birth of the Sandinista Front. Of the three founders, only Tomás Borge is still alive, but the face of Carlos Fonseca, the fighter and theoretician, is a familiar image in Nicaragua today. Fonseca had been involved in fighting before the foundation of the Front; in 1959 he was wounded while other students, peasants and workers of their guerrilla group were gunned down in a National Guard ambush. When students in León marched in protest against the massacre they were also met with bullets.

The event was formative for a generation of young men and women such as Rosario Antunes Borjas (*q.v.*), but during the sixties the Sandinistas were still a tiny group, organising clandestine city cells and mountain guerrilla units in the Pacific region. In the seventies the FSLN gathered strength, and the National Guard responded with increasing brutality. Many of the Guard rank and file were themselves poor peasants and workers who had been pressganged into the military, where they were trained to terrorise the people, to silence them through fear. As a Sandinista once said to Carmen López (*q.v.*), 'to be young today in Nicaragua is dangerous'; the Guard would pick up and torture a young man in the street just, as Nicaraguans would say, *por gusto*, for the hell of it.

But the Sandinistas' audacity in confronting this repression, and the alternative vision of society which they offered, drew people into the FSLN. School and university students came into contact with underground organisers; people of all ages, especially women, were politicised by the radical theology of progressive priests and nuns. For young urban workers and the unemployed there was little left to lose. Their mothers, faced with the murder and mutilation of their children, began to organise against the Guard, and if their sons and daughters were involved with the Sandinistas their protective maternal role became political. One-third of the FSLN fighting force was female, and it was the women who formed the basis of the support networks, without which the guerrillas could not operate. They provided food, bought medicines, ran first-aid posts, sewed uniforms, made their houses 'safe' for Sandinistas to hide, and carried messages – and arms – in their market baskets.

The middle classes too, became disaffected by Somoza's corruption and the privileges of his exclusive clique, and as the open battle with the Guard spread across the country, they saw in the armed FSLN the only hope of ending the regime. Even the official church hierarchy, now openly anti-Sandinista, sanctioned the use of force against the dictatorship at that time, and men and women from all sections of society joined in the general strike six weeks before Somoza fell.

But it was the youth of the *barrios* who fired from behind the barricades in the popular insurrections. At the end of June 1979 the FSLN withdrew their forces from Managua, marching to nearby Masaya during the night to wait for the final moment. Cities were falling to the Sandinistas, the people erupted in Managua, and when the guerrillas converged on the capital on 19 July, Somoza had fled and the Guard disintegrated. In America's post-Vietnam climate of concern for human rights, President

Carter could not continue to support the regime. He hoped to stave off real revolution by selecting Somoza's successor, but the Sandinistas swept unopposed into Managua amidst a storm of celebrations.

Despite their joy at what Nicaraguans call 'the triumph', the country was in chaos. The banks were empty, the economy in ruins and the FSLN victorious but inexperienced. Their assets were idealism, enormous energy and an intimate knowledge of the Pacific region through their guerrilla life amongst the people. Daniel Ortega, elected president in 1984, together with the other eight members of the Sandinista directorate, had been a commander of FSLN forces.

During the years which have followed the triumph, the Sandinistas have stuck to their own brand of socialism: the principle of government for the poor rather than the privileged, and by the people rather than a ruling class. These theories develop through practice rather than rigid political positions; Sandinista policy is to learn through trial and, as they themselves admit, through error.

A top priority in economic reconstruction, beside the need to restore production, was to deal with the problems of unemployment and of landlessness. Initially the emphasis was on the creation of large state farms from Somoza's properties, which had made up more than 20 per cent of all arable land. But because Nicaragua has a mixed economy, with both public and private ownership, this could not provide the sole model for development. The state now controls all exports, but 60 per cent of production in this sector is still in private hands. Many large landowners who farm efficiently and respect the National Union of Agricultural Workers (ATC) have kept part or all of their lands. The majority in the private sector are, however, medium- or small-scale farmers, and it is they who grow 75 per cent of food for home consumption and 40 per cent of export crops. For the first time credit and technical assistance have been made available to these producers, who also now have their own union, the National Association of Farmers and Ranchers (UNAG), which encourages the creation of co-operatives. Most co-ops are based on shared services for individual farms, but in a small though increasing number, like El Regadío (pp. 93–94), the land is held in common and farmed collectively.

Despite its importance, UNAG does not define the relationship between small farmer and the state. The organisation itself responds to pressure from below, and it has been the popular demand for land which has shaped Agrarian Reform since 1984. Existing land use has been recognised by legal titles and land from both private and state farms given to individual producers. There is also a new recognition of the *campesina*; by law women may now own land, and although this has yet to be achieved, they should be fully integrated into co-operatives on equal terms with men.

The FSLN has won rural political support through this new emphasis on the subsistence sector, the small producer and the rights of women farmers. But 20 per cent of the rural population still has no land; some large landowners are feeling threatened, and class conflict rankles in the countryside. As conditions there improve, and *campesinos* are paid more for their produce, town dwellers complain of shortages, rising prices and distribution bottlenecks. Another problem arising from increased land ownership and rural security, plus the demands of national defence, is a shortage of seasonal labour. Now volunteer brigades pick the coffee and the cotton: students and teachers, workers and professionals, together with international teams, mix with waged labour on the estates. Many are shocked by what they find there: the dark one-roomed dwellings for the permanent workers' families; the wide wooden bunks on which the seasonal labourers sleep. This first-hand experience of rural conditions breaks down barriers not only between classes but also between town and country.

The cornerstone of this development was the Literacy

Crusade. In 1980, 85,000 schoolchildren and students left the towns to live alongside *campesinos*, sharing their food, work, discomfort and rudimentary housing whilst teaching them to read and write. In less than six months, national illiteracy was lowered from 50 per cent to 12 per cent, and a generation of young people experienced a profound political education richer than any revolutionary rhetoric. Over half of the *brigadistas* were young girls. Away from home, fending for themselves and mixing freely and equally with boys, many felt their lives transformed. Health campaigns have been conducted along the same lines. Besides building new hospitals, rural clinics and centres for children dehydrated by diarrhoea, teams of briefly trained voluntary *brigadistas* have taken basic health care and education to the remotest regions. Nicaragua's health service is hamstrung by shortages of skills, supplies and equipment, and by conservatism among the older professionals, but the preventative approach has had spectacular results. Through the volunteer immunisation campaigns, polio has been completely eradicated, and infant mortality reduced to 7 per cent.

Social programmes cannot depend primarily on professionals and high technology; there is in Nicaragua neither the personnel nor the resources. But more than this, community self-reliance is a basic principle of the revolution. The FSLN sees people as agents of social change, not simply as recipients. Popular participation gives people a stake in the society they are creating and exposes them to new experience.

The main agents of popular democracy are the mass organisations, associations of different sections of society: the neighbourhood committees (CDS), the Labour union (CST), the ATC, UNAG, the women's association (AMNLAE), the teachers' union, the Sandinista Youth and the children's organisation. All have similar structures, with local, regional and national committees, and thus have influence at the level of the state. Some are strong and influential, others less so. Some are also strikingly

independent. Critics claim that mass organisations serve primarily as arms of the Sandinista Party, and with the wartime needs of security and national cohesion, this did seem possible. But, in practice, the organisations respond both to direction from above and to pressure from below, a two-way dialogue that both implements FSLN policy and shapes it. UNAG provides one example of this process; AMNLAE provides another.

Women and Revolution

The FSLN was committed to women's equality from the start. 'Women will be given a more dignified place in society,' stated its programme, 'and all their rights in society will be enforced so that they are not subject to discrimination'. But when foreign feminists first visited AMNLAE, Nicaraguan priorities were made very clear: national reconstruction before all else; women's particular problems would have to wait. Women must integrate into the revolution, support its projects, participate in national defence, and not raise issues that could be divisive. Through this active involvement women would be liberated.

In one sense AMNLAE was right. The revolution was under threat, and without it women would get nowhere. Many of the improvements which appeared to be of general social benefit – health, housing, education – were in fact of particular value to women because of their family responsibilities. AMNLAE did ensure, moreover, that women participated in these projects both as beneficiaries and as agents. And as the women talking in this book reveal, it has been through their active involvement with the FSLN, the militia, neighbourhood committees, the Literacy Campaign and so on that they have become conscious of their own potential and gained the confidence to realise it. How else would they have had the courage, or opportunity, to emerge from backgrounds of rural poverty to travel to Mexico to acquire expertise in herbal medicines; to work in a printing press; to write and broadcast for a union; to head a section of the ATC? They all speak of the space which the revolution has given women to grow and develop: 'I've woken up at last,' says Otilia Casco Cruz (*q.v.*). What else could have fed her poetic imagination to express her new perceptions?

Nevertheless, as part of its original platform, AMNLAE did also tackle aspects of women's specific oppression, especially through legal reform, so increasing consciousness of women's demands and opening the way for further action. First, the exploitation of women as sexual objects in commercial advertising was prohibited. Then the maintenance law ruled that a father must contribute financially towards his child, even if not living with the mother. This law has its limitations – if a man is self-employed or has no work, for example, his pay cannot be docked at source; some women, too, prefer to be self-sufficient. But the principle of paternal responsibility is there, as it is also in the law which stipulates equality between family members in the home, including the sharing of domestic labour. When parents separate, mothers now usually gain custody of their children, whereas before the revolution all rights lay with the father.

AMNLAE, however, did not at first seem to gain the popular support it had hoped for. So in 1984, to help determine future directions, it called meetings in different neighbourhoods to listen to women's problems rather than to tell women what their priorities should be.

And what did AMNLAE discover? Women did not talk about production, health campaigns or their children's education, but about rape, domestic violence, sexual harassment, alcoholism, *machismo*, birth control, sex education and abortion. At its National Assembly the following year, these issues dominated the debate. When FSLN Commander Bayardo Arce spoke, congratulating the women on their revolutionary spirit and for keeping the home fires burning while their menfolk fought the war, he was challenged. Women told him they needed no patronage from men and that the Party must now take on board women's demands. Those who spoke out were not educated AMNLAE officials but workers like Flor Ramírez (*q.v.*) who are increasingly prepared to confront the authority not only of their husbands but also of Sandinista officials.

Implementation of this new direction will be difficult. *Machismo* does not die overnight, and resistance to these demands occurs at every level, from debates in the higher echelons of the FSLN to kitchen confrontations between wife and husband. As the lives of the women in this book show, the personal cost of freedom can be high, both in terms of rupture of relationships and of endless work. Then over everything hangs the menace of US aggression, draining resources and energies away from realising ideals. But in spite of conflicting national priorities and the pressure of defence, what we might call feminist demands are on the agenda.

The war itself has also generated change. Although there are now few women in the army, they form the great majority in civil defence. They are also moving into traditional male employment as men are called up to fight. The female tractor drivers in Jalapa set a precedent that many others have followed, and have reinforced the ATC's platform of equal rights at work. AMNLAE also continues to organise around the political dimensions of motherhood. The Patriotic Front of Mothers and Relatives supports those who leave home for military service; the Association of Mothers of Heroes and Martyrs brings together those whose children never come back. On a personal level, mothers need mutual support when members of their family leave to fight the war against the Contra, and when they die, seek comfort and a meaning for their grief from those who have also experienced this bitter loss.

US Aggression against Nicaragua

By September 1986 the Contra war against the Sandinistas had claimed 34,000 casualties; that is, 1 per cent of the total population killed, wounded, kidnapped or disappeared. Over a quarter of a million people have been driven from their homes, and whole communities have had to resettle in safer zones. Although the most publicised resettlement has been on the Atlantic Coast, on the Pacific side of the country people in the northern and central regions have been pushed from their communities as bands of Contra have emerged from their Honduran bases or from camps deep inside the Nicaraguan countryside to rape, murder and terrorise by the most horrific forms of torture. It is these men whom President Reagan refers to as 'freedom fighters'.

Many of the Contra are *campesinos* kidnapped during these raids. Others are ex-Somoza National Guard who either fled from Nicaragua when the FSLN came to power, or who left later when released from jail. Although many Nicaraguans would like to see the Guard pay for what they did, the FSLN has pursued a non-retributive policy towards the ex-Guard, just as they now offer amnesty to all Contra who hand in their arms. The Miami-based leaders of the main Contra organisation, the Nicaraguan Democratic Front (FDN) served under Somoza, while the other main group, the Democratic Revolutionary Alliance (ARDE), was founded by a disaffected Sandinista Commander, Eden Pastora. ARDE, which operated from Costa Rica, has now disintegrated, but there are still some 10,000 Contra under arms.

Their atrocities have been aimed particularly at those connected with the revolution: agricultural advisers, health *brigadistas*, adult education organisers. Co-op members work with guns slung on their backs; international volunteers have been attacked; co-op buildings, schools and rural clinics have been reduced to rubble; roads, bridges, electrical plants and other economic targets have been destroyed. In 1983 the fuel storage tanks in the port of Corinto were blown up, and the following year Nicaragua's four principal harbours were mined. This was too much even for the US Congress, and although (as became very clear in 1986) covert action continued unabated, the CIA were banned from involvement in the war.

The economic cost of Contra campaigns is crippling: $2,500 million in physical destruction and lost production. In 1986 direct and indirect damage represented 60 per cent of the country's export earnings. Like all Central American states, Nicaragua is suffering from the collapse of agro-export prices in the world market. But unlike her neighbours, who are flooded with US assistance, Nicaragua has been faced with the gradual withdrawal of both aid and access to US markets, with a total trade embargo in 1985. American-made machines lie idle with no spare parts; shops are empty of imported goods that Nicaragua's own small manufacturing sector cannot supply. Not only has bilateral aid been cut off, but Reagan puts pressure on multilateral agencies such as the Inter-American Development Bank to end all credit to Nicaragua. In 1986 Congress not only approved a multi-million-dollar aid package to the Contra, but reauthorised the CIA to intervene. This meant that the $400 million already earmarked for covert operations could now openly be used for Contra backing.

Why is Reagan determined to bring down the Sandinistas? What threat does such a small country offer to a superpower? Reagan's explanation is that he is helping restore democracy to a people crushed by a Marxist-Leninist regime; the US press turns out stories of censorship, religious persecution, human rights abuse, and a state security system that forces Nicaraguans to live in fear. Using cold war rhetoric, Reagan characterises Central American guerrilla struggles such as those in Guatemala and El Salvador as a response not to years of poverty and repression, but to communist provocation.

But long before the foundation of the FSLN, control of

Nicaragua was central to US domination of the region. The country is important economically and under Somoza the US controlled 70 per cent of foreign investment and monopolised Nicaragua's markets. But the real significance of this country with both Pacific and Atlantic coasts is strategic, not only to control the vulnerable Caribbean basin, but as a springboard for US troops used to bring down the reformist government of Guatemala in 1954, the popular Dominican Republic regime in 1965 and to attack Cuba with the Bay of Pigs in 1961. The US cannot tolerate an independent state in its back yard, particularly if it threatens to be successful. Revolutions are not exportable. But the example of Nicaragua gives hope and confidence to other Latin American movements fighting for social justice.

One option for the United States would be direct assault. Nicaragua has expected this since the invasion of Grenada in 1983 and remains prepared. But, as in the past, the US prefers to let others do the fighting while it manoeuvres behind the scenes. Allies exist inside the country, not only in the Contra but among sections of the middle classes whose opposition is orchestrated by the upper echelons of the church. By exacerbating internal conflicts, destabilising the economy and disrupting social life, Nicaragua will, it is hoped, be brought to the brink of bankruptcy and support for the FSLN destroyed. This policy has had some success. There are very serious economic problems: soaring inflation, the dearth of foreign exchange, rising prices and shortages of goods cause discontent among a hard-pressed people. The cost of defence, over half the national budget, diverts resources from social programmes that Nicaraguans now expect. As far as possible, volunteers protect their own communities with local militia, night-watch duty and civil defence. But the army has to be maintained while National Service takes young workers out of production. The government is widely held responsible for the hardship, and grumblings about the FSLN increase.

But what the United States does not understand is the difference between criticism and counter-revolution. A people which has survived Somoza, a civil war and the devastating earthquake of 1972 which destroyed the capital will not easily surrender to a foreign power. Nor are mercenaries and kidnapped conscripts a match for what a popular slogan calls 'a people in arms' – a people who have taken control of their own history and will not now hand it back.

One long-term US aim has been to secure a base in Nicaragua, to control an area in which to set up an opposition government. But the Contra have failed to hold a single town for any length of time, even in the target area – the vulnerable Atlantic Coast.

The Atlantic Coast

The term 'Atlantic Coast' is misleading. Zelaya, as the region is called, is not just a strip of coast, but extends far inwards from the seaboard to cover half the national territory. Yet *The Tiger's Milk* is unusual in opening with a section on the Coast, for writers on Nicaragua often merely refer in passing to the region or confine it to footnotes. Its distinct history makes it difficult to tie in with accounts of the Pacific where the Sandinista struggle was born, the revolution was shaped and which has become synonymous with 'Nicaragua'. Zelaya's differences from the Pacific – geographical, historical, ethnic, linguistic, political, and in its religious affiliations – set it apart. When you come to the end of the long journey from Managua, winding by boat along the river to Bluefields, or you step off the small plane that skims over miles of impenetrable tropical forest, you feel as if you are in a different country. The hot steamy climate and perpetual rain, the small stilted houses in palm-fringed villages, the isolated communities reached only by boat, have little in common with what you have left behind. Flat plainlands feature in parts of both areas, but while the *leit-motif* of the Pacific is volcanoes and mountains, on the Coast it is water – streams, rivers, lagoons, swamps and the sea itself.

Marginalised in the past, the Atlantic Coast is now a central issue because of both the self-assertion of the *costeño*, coastal people, and manipulation of this by the United States. But the particular character and history of the Coast are constantly mentioned by those speaking in this book because they are crucial to an understanding of the complex nature of the region's politics.

Only 10 per cent of Nicaraguans live in Zelaya, but they include a wide variety of ethnic groups, each with its own language. Current US propaganda gives the impression that the Coast is peopled entirely by Indians, but the majority of the population here, as throughout Nicaragua, is in fact Mestizo. The culture of the northern Zelaya region, however, is dominated by the Miskito Indians, who make up one third of the coastal population. In the south, it is the Creoles who predominate, Afro-European descendants of black labour imported from Africa and the Caribbean by the British and North Americans. The two main port towns on the Coast, southern Bluefields and Puerto Cabezas in the north, also have a strong Creole character, but although four of the people speaking in this book are Creole, they comprise only 10 per cent of all *costeños*. The remaining representative of the Coast in the book, Dionisia López (*q.v.*), is from the small community of Sumu Indians; Rama Indians and Garifunas are even fewer in number.

Before the British pirates and traders arrived on the Coast in the seventeenth century, the population was mainly Sumu. One Indian group, who came to be called Miskito, attempted to avoid the decimation that indigenous peoples had suffered on the Pacific side and allied themselves with the newcomers. Later in the century, the British created and crowned a Miskito 'king' who ensured colonial control, and with the aid of newly acquired firearms and local political power, the Miskito asserted their dominance over the Sumus, who retreated,

preserving their culture but not their numbers. Ironically, although the US now paints a picture of a rich indigenous tradition raped by Sandinista forces, the Miskito owe not only much of their culture, but also their very existence to British intervention.

Miskito reliance on foreign powers is thus an historical inheritance. Another is their hostility to the Pacific. During the sixteenth and seventeenth centuries the British used the Miskito to fight their colonial wars against the settlers from Spain, preventing their expansion to the Coast and exacerbating Miskito hatred of the 'Spanish', a term still used today for the Mestizos.

At the end of the nineteenth century, when British interests had declined, the ruling president, Zelaya, deposed the Miskito king and incorporated the region into Nicaragua, giving the new department his name. These actions were deeply resented by the *costeños*, for although the British had exploited both resources and labour through lumber and sugar enterprises, it was only the 'Spanish' who were seen as foreign invaders. Similarly, although North America exerted domination from the 1880s, exporting the profits from rubber, timber, bananas and gold straight to the United States, *costeños* like Helena Williams and Doris Gabay (*q.v.*) tend to recall the health services the Americans provided and the 'good old days' of imported goods in the company stores. By 1979, the Coast had been stripped of many of its natural resources and many companies had left, yet resentment was aimed rather at the Managuan government who raked off the companies' concessions but did little for the Coast.

Hostilities were also directed inwards through another legacy – the racist stereotypes of a class-race hierarchy created by colonialism. The Miskito were considered inferior and 'primitive' not only by the white expatriates, but by the Creoles who were educated into European culture for administrative posts. Doris Gabay (*q.v.*) sums it up: whites had Creole servants; Creoles had Miskito. The Miskito thus resented Creoles and the social and economic marginalisation that all Indians had suffered. Despite this, there is a deep-rooted inter-indigenous conflict between Miskito Indians and the Sumu and Rama who come at the bottom of the ladder. As for the coastal Mestizo, peasants and landless labourers are looked down upon while those with education share the sense of superiority of their Pacific counterparts. For during Somoza's regime, the Pacific population, informed primarily by prejudice about a region that few had visited, despised *costeños* of whatever origin.

This was the situation inherited, although little understood, by the Sandinistas in 1979. There were only a handful of Creoles and even fewer Miskito in the FSLN, and for many people on the Coast it was hard to celebrate the end of a brutal dictatorship when the National Guard had hardly appeared in the area, when local participation in the struggle had been minimal and where some remote communities had never even heard Somoza's name. FSLN slogans and symbols had little resonance on the Coast, for Sandino, who attacked banana plantations in the thirties, was not seen as a national hero, and the predominant ideology on the Coast was not anti-imperialism, but anti-communism, US-style.

The FSLN were committed in their original programme to developing the region and integrating the Coast into the revolutionary project. But the model for their plans was based on the class conflict of the Pacific rather than the ethnic contradictions of the Coast. For example, some of the agricultural schemes for small producers promoted by Pacific officials were inappropriate for Miskito, accustomed to community landholding and collective self-help, and they felt threatened by these 'Spanish' innovations.

The Sandinistas were aware, however, that Zelaya had special needs, and as on the Pacific the principle of popular participation provided the space for minority demands. Whereas an earlier Indian organisation, the Alliance for the Progress of Miskito and Sumu people

(ALPROMISU), had been neutralised by Somoza's interference, its replacement, MISURASATA (union of Miskito, Sumu, Rama and Sandinista), founded late in 1979, was supported by the FSLN as a mass organisation, and given a free hand to operate. The leaders were young university-educated Miskito: Hazel Lau (*q.v.*), Brooklyn Rivera and Steadman Fagoth. Their chief concern was not involvement in the revolution but the historic demands of the Miskito people. When coupled with charisma and great personal ambition, as in the case of the two men, this led to the development of a popular opposition movement to the FSLN. When MISURASATA was given control of the coastal literacy campaign in local languages, they used it as a platform to undermine the government and consolidate their own position. When Fagoth was made responsible for the survey to determine indigenous land rights, his demands amounted to a territorial base for Miskito separatism. The Sandinistas, startled by their popular support, jailed a number of MISURASATA leaders in early 1981. Even though Fagoth was by now publicly known as a former Somoza security agent, he had a great following, and the effect of his imprisonment was to strengthen the movement rather than to weaken it.

The United States, with its long contact with the Coast and experience elsewhere of manipulating ethnic rivalries, was quick to realise that this region was the Achilles heel of the revolution. MISURASATA leaders were soon on the CIA payroll, and by mid-1981 Fagoth was out of prison and based in a Honduran training camp with several thousand Miskito followers. Now allied with the Contra FDN, Fagoth renamed his force MISURA, while Brooklyn Rivera took MISURASATA to Costa Rica to link up with ARDE.

At the end of the year, after months of MISURA attacks, the FSLN learned of Fagoth's ambitious plan, known as Red Christmas, to provoke insurrection among the Miskito communities along the River Coco which divides Honduras from Nicaragua, declare a liberated zone, and establish a US-backed provisional government. In January 1982, the FSLN rapidly removed 8,000 Miskito from this area, and resettled them further south in Tasba Pri (Free Land). In the wake of the exodus, their houses, crops and animals were destroyed to prevent the Contra from using their villages as a base. Although resources were poured into the new settlements, the move caused great distress. The FSLN now acknowledge that mistakes made in their handling of this situation, as others in this period, fuelled fear of the Sandinistas on the Coast. Some young and inexperienced soldiers, ignorant of coastal cultures and afraid of people whose language they did not understand, lacked respect and discipline. An obsession with security and the search for informers led to abuses of human rights. But the FSLN had cause to worry. Collaboration with the Contra, whether through conviction, confusion or force, was widespread, and included some Creoles, and by 1985 over a quarter of all active Contra were Miskito Indians.

The targets for Contra action are similar to those on the Pacific, and the attacks have been equally brutal. Both individuals and communities, often uninvolved themselves, have been forced to move, and this has hit particularly hard at women with their family responsibilities. Both fear and force have driven many to refugee camps in Honduras.

North American influence in the war has also been exerted through the hegemony of the Moravian Church among the deeply religious peoples of the Coast. When the Protestant Moravians arrived from Germany in 1849, the Miskito espoused the church both as a means of advancement and as an alternative to 'Spanish' Catholicism. Today, even though it is now run from the United States, it is more of a local religion than a missionary church. The Moravians have been the principal providers of whatever social services have existed, and the pastor, appointed from the locality, is the focus of community life. Creoles also practise other forms of Protestantism which, by promoting hopes in the hereafter rather than the present, provides yet more scope for anti-communist propaganda.

Although the Moravian Church is politically divided, its leader, Andy Shogreen (q.v.), is somewhat disingenuous when he speaks in this book of the church's role as intermediary between government and people. Many pastors who feel their position threatened by the rival power of the FSLN have relied heavily on US funding and are seen as openly sympathetic to the opposition movements. As on the Pacific, FSLN conflict with sections of the church makes their work more difficult.

FSLN Response and Autonomy for the Atlantic Coast

As in every area, the FSLN have learned through their experience. They have deepened their understanding of the complexities of the Coast, and worked to dispel mistrust. The army, which now incorporates battalions of local volunteers, is better informed and disciplined. *Costeños* have also been appointed to official positions at all levels, among them Hazel Lau (q.v.), now FSLN representative of Northern Zelaya to the National Assembly. Despite lack of personnel and resources, the difficulties of communication and the problems caused by the war, social and economic projects have gone ahead. Primary education is now to be conducted in the mother tongue instead of Spanish, and so no longer discriminates against the non-Mestizo child. Agricultural and fishing developments range from large-scale projects to assistance for small producers and collectives. The first road and telephone links now join the two sections of the country, and the Sandinistas promote Coastal culture as part of the national heritage.

These projects aim to promote peace by providing proof of Sandinista good intentions and the well-being of the people. But a prerequisite for their success is peace. For example, health programmes include both the building of new hospitals and preventative and curative care in the communities, but many rural health centres have been destroyed by Contra action.

Peace is also vital for the area's single most important project – that of self-government for the Coast. The FSLN published the first draft of the autonomy proposals in 1985 at the same time as signing a ceasefire with opposition groups. This was followed by months of discussion at village and regional level throughout the area, involving the communities in planning for their future, and pilot projects around some of the proposals are now under way.

Autonomy means different things to different people, and details of its final form will evolve in practice. But to everyone on the Coast it holds out the hope of exercising political rights and confirming their cultural identity. Through their local committees and the two regional assemblies of northern and southern Zelaya, *costeños* will participate in the planning and implementation of local economic, social and cultural development. Traditional land rights, both individual and collective, will be recognised, and communities will receive the major benefit from the exploitation of natural resources on their land. The assemblies will have a role in the legal process of their region, and their members will be elected by the people.

The aim of autonomy is to consolidate the nation, not to fragment it, and the state will retain overall control of defence, security, economic planning and foreign policy. But Nicaragua itself is now defined as a unity of various cultures, each to be protected and promoted through regional self-government.

This is unique in Latin America where indigenous peoples have been marginalised both by the right, through exploitation and genocide, and by a left which often argues that ethnic identity is secondary to class struggle. Autonomy is thus doubly dangerous to the United States, for it offers the end of conflict on the Atlantic Coast and sets a precedent for struggles elsewhere. As a result, efforts to discredit the Sandinistas and destabilise the region have intensified, and money and military assistance to the Miskito Contra have increased.

However, the opposition is not united. The FDN-promoted Miskito group, Kisan, has split in two: 'Kisan for War' is still fighting from Honduras, but 'Kisan for Peace' is participating in autonomy negotiations with the FSLN. Similarly, although coastal communities are still deeply divided, both inside and between themselves, the obvious self-interest of Fagoth and Rivera, and the violence and terror they have engendered, have cost them support. People are sick of the war and are pressing for peace.

The River Coco remains an unsettled area. Many Miskito returned from the Tasba Pri and from Honduras during the autonomy discussions; some of them left again for Honduras and are now coming back once more.

Despite uncertainties, the autonomy process has proved the Sandinista's sincerity. *Costeños* are beginning to realise that the apparent deep concern of the US for indigenous and minority rights is hardly born out by history, and that they may have more to hope from the FSLN.

The Tiger's Milk

This book, then, is not only about women, it is an exploration of the search for an identity, a voice, by people who for too long have been unrecognised and silent – peasant farmers, indigenous and ethnic communities, and women. In each case the FSLN set out with a programme to end discrimination and open a space for popular initiative, but in practice national interests at first took precedence over sectional demands. But with the new confidence gained from recognition, the people themselves began to state their own problems. The FSLN listened, deepened their understanding of the issues, and acted upon them.

Alicia Andino (*q.v.*) says, 'the revolution is what we make it', and women have been crucial in this process. Fiona

Macintosh and Adriana Angel do not claim that the testimonies of *The Tiger's Milk* reflect the majority opinion among women in Nicaragua. But those women who do become alive to their oppression and to the possibility of change have, through their participation in the revolution, come to identify with the whole of Nicaraguan society. To focus on this is not just hopeful romanticism about a revolution. For most of us in the west, pursuing our own concerns in a materialistic, individualistic and highly competitive society, such commitment may be hard to understand. But for many Nicaraguans today, life has little meaning outside the interests of their community and country. Despite their inevitable frustrations, the political determination of those who have made the leap is matched by great personal feeling. When Rosario Antunes Borjas (*q.v.*) first made contact with the FSLN she felt 'a total happiness – I imagined it was like falling deeply in love.'

To begin with the intricacies of the Atlantic Coast in a book dedicated to these themes may at first seem confusing. However, the history of the Atlantic region is not there only to give insight into particular women's lives but to give a fuller picture of Nicaraguan society and of the assaults upon it. *The Tiger's Milk* charts a journey, a voyage which would not be complete without the Coast. First, the contrast between the Atlantic and Pacific shows one area on the verge of change and the other more dramatically transformed. Secondly, the testimonies themselves mark different stages of the journey as we start from detached passivity and resignation, explore the gaining of social conscience and self-awareness, and arrive at commitment to the revolution and to change. Thirdly, this progress is charted within individual consciousness as the speakers describe their difficult and uneven paths to different views of self and of the world.

Beginning the book with discussion of the Atlantic Coast also illustrates both the enormous difficulties which the Sandinistas face and the complexity of the situation which they inherited. It shows what a long, slow and painful

process a revolution is. For, contrary to the impression given by some well-meaning but, I believe, misguided films and books on Nicaragua, a revolution does not automatically pour out a cornucopia of co-operatives, health campaigns, women's collectives, literacy classes, childcare centres and clinics. These things have been created by the people, but they struggle for survival not only against lack of resources, vested interests and the devastation of war, but also against apathy, suspicion, inexperience and personal idiosyncracies. All too often those involved in dramatic social change are portrayed as neat packages of political resolve and unflagging activity, all rough edges burnt away in the heat of revolutionary fervour. Some of the interviews in this book do reflect the rhetoric with which committed people speak, but in real life people remain untidy and complex human beings, in conflict not only with each other, but often within themselves.

But what also emerges is the true transformation that a revolution brings: the dedication it inspires, the energies it releases, the barriers it breaks. As these speaking here constantly claim, the Nicaraguan revolution has opened a space for people to realise themselves as never before. As the book shows, some enter into this space; others, through history or personal circumstance, hold back. But the opportunity is there.

What the assault on Nicaragua means is a threat to close that space, dam that energy, and force the majority of men and women back into the vicious circle of poverty and passivity on which domination depends.

Hermione Harris,
London, 1986

Authors' preface

We came to Nicaragua following the 1979 revolution which brought the Sandinista government to power. At first we lived in the capital, Managua, but life there gave us only a partial view of the enormous changes happening in the country at large. So early in 1984 we began travelling, and as we made our way back and forth across the country we interviewed and photographed peasants, politicians, teachers, trade unionists, mothers, midwives and factory workers who were willing to share their time and thoughts with us. It is these people, nearly all of them women, who are the subject of *The Tiger's Milk*.

Our aim was not to construct an encyclopaedic overview of the lives of all Nicaraguan women, who together might represent all shades of opinion and class. Rather, we wanted to learn something of the inner thoughts, motivations and actions of a range of people whose lives have been affected, more or less dramatically, by the revolution. For it is the very personal quality of commitment to change which lies at the heart of the country's revolutionary politics.

Only at the end of our travels did the book's structure emerge. Essentially, it reflects a society in transition, from a history of foreign domination and the loss of cultural identity to the achievement of individual and collective emancipation within a democratic society. Rosario Antunes, the last speaker in the book, describes this collective effort as a deep love for life, symbolised in the fable of the tiger's milk, which expresses the inner confidence of the individual to transform society. The book, we hope, describes this process, as women leave behind isolation and passive acceptance of domination to join in a common effort to confront and change society.

In dedicating this book to the people of Nicaragua we will be giving our authors' payments to women's projects in Nicaragua.

Acknowledgements

We wish to thank all those who gave us support and encouragement to produce this book and in particular those people whose testimonies appear in it: Dionisia Frank López, Rafael Dixon, Helena Williams, Doris Gabay, Andy Shogreen, Alta Hooker, Mildred Levy, Hazel Lau, Verónica Gonzales, Rita López, Lesbia Joya Diaz, Wilfredo Joya Diaz, José María Briones, Adela Cruz, Otilia Casco Cruz, Tacho Olivas Cruz, María del Carmen López Calero, Alicia Andino, Victoria Torres, Flor Ramírez, María Borjas, Rosario Antunes Borjas.

We are also deeply grateful for the support given to us by Christian Aid, London.

THE ATLANTIC COAST

A SEARCH FOR PEACE

Dionisia Frank López

A Sumu Indian who, following counter-revolutionary incursions, was forced to leave her community on the River Coco, which divides Nicaragua and Honduras. She is at present living in Rosita.

We used to live well along the River Coco. We fished and found all we needed. The men hunted deer, wild pig and birds; we grew rice, beans, cassava root, bananas, oranges, coconut and sugar cane as well. The bananas were so big that the women couldn't carry them. I used to carry up to 100 pounds, but since I had my six children I've been able to lift only 70 pounds. We built our own homes with wood and zinc, and sometimes with bamboo. The women plaited palm leaves to make the roofs; we made blankets from tuno bark, baskets from reeds, and clay pots. The mothers with small babies would stay at home. The others helped the men fish and plant rice and maize, while their children cared for the smaller ones; then at midday the women would return to cook.

Here in Rosita we don't have any good land. It's difficult. When you have no money you have no food. But if we went back to the river with all the other people we'd have to start all over again and we don't want to go yet. We have all our things here and the children are at school. I miss the river and my friends who've returned, but we're all right here. It's a hard life with the four families in the one house, but we'll wait a little longer. Things done in haste turn out badly.[1]

We came first to La Españolina, but moved to Rosita when a family was murdered. After this many other families also moved away to Tasba Pri, the Sumubila settlement, where they felt safer. What happened was that the men were drinking their *chicha* [maize beer] through the night (they're always drunk on a Sunday) down at the other community, and a man started a fight with one of our men. He left to get his gun and came to find our man, Suayerno, who'd returned home. There he shot Suayerno and his wife and three other people – only their children escaped. The bullets flew over my brother's bed – but God is powerful: we managed to run for cover.

All this for drinking! They say to stop a man you need to make him drink the milk from a black pig. There used to be none of this fighting and drinking. We had our festivals, we'd prepare pig and river fish, cook tortillas and cheese and buy some flour. The church celebrated the birth of Christ and taught the children to sing hymns to the Lord. But in Españolina there were no festivals, only drinking. For years we lived near to the Miskitos along the river, but this killing never happened in my generation.

For sure the Miskitos don't like us. We should be able to live together because the land is for everyone, but the Miskitos don't think so. They say the Sumus are worthless. In the past they killed our men for their land, they pushed

A displaced Sumu Indian family in La Españolina.

The Sumu Indian community of La Españolina

us out and there became too few of us to fight back. Now there are more Miskitos than us. We let them work beside us and we say nothing. They buy our produce, but only if they can get it cheap; yet they sell their clothes at such high prices that we're still in the same clothes we brought with us from the river five years ago. The Miskitos are different from us. They make such a noise over the smallest thing; like the women will even come to blows over a man. We women would never fight over a man. The Miskito men don't respect their women or children. If we have to punish a child it's with two slaps and a talking to. We show them that it is wrong to fight, or to tell lies and steal, and that they must respect their elders. The elders counsel the young as they're wise, and are listened to.

[1]We visited the Atlantic Coast and spoke to Dionisia Frank López and the other people in this chapter in 1985, during a ceasefire with one of the rebel forces, MISURA. This permitted many of the war-displaced people in North Zelaya to return home. Yet rebel incursions do continue to disrupt the people's efforts to rebuild their communities on the River Coco.

Rafael Dixon

A Miskito Moravian Church minister who returned to his River Coco town of Waspan during the 1985 ceasefire. The town was destroyed in 1982 during rebel force activities, so the government relocated the people to safer ground.

For me the best woman to marry is one who works, because she brings in the money. Some women are so good with the machete that they can cut down more bush than their men. The woman wakes first to cook, then she goes with her man to the fields. When they return she does the housework and prepares the food for her husband; then she gathers up the dirty clothes to wash them in the river, returns home, cleans the house and prepares the food. It strikes me that we men are lazier than the women because they chop the wood, carry in the bananas and do

Miskito Indians return to their communities during the 1985 ceasefire

the heavy jobs. The man only carries his machete and banana pole. When he comes in from the fields he just goes and rests in the hammock. She doesn't say anything, it's the man who gives the orders, and after he's eaten then he sleeps with his lady. If a man has money it's because his woman helps him. This is true all over Nicaragua.

In Managua the men are out drinking while the women are busy working. Well, here we have no entertainment so our only enjoyment is to raise children and that's why not a year passes without the woman pregnant. Before '82 we used to have two cinemas, two restaurants and the Star restaurant in Waspan. I've never been drunk or danced a step. My only pleasures have been women and work, and because of this I have lots of children – but then I also have five women and they all keep me. They all have their work – some sell bread – and my official wife takes the children to school in Puerto Cabezas to complete their primary and secondary education while the other women work on the land and breed the pigs. They keep me and help me.

Well, yes, there are problems. If you want to have two or three women you need to have a very big heart, because when they hit you and get you on the floor and beat you up you have to have patience. At times they've wanted to kill me, but if I'm dead who will give them a kiss in the morning? I'd be a rotten corpse and have to be buried. Ah, I'm very bad, as they say, but all over the world men have more than two women. Even ministers like me.

A Miskito woman cleaning rice

Helena Williams

A Miskito midwife from the Miskito Wawa community on the Karata Lagoon, not far from Puerto Cabezas (Port).

My mother was Miskito and my father North American. He met her here, while felling mahogany for the United States. My mother was fine and dark, and that is how I came out too. But now my grandchildren are blond and fair-skinned, because of my father. Mother gave me everything she could. I was happy. She gave me shoes and clothes and I went to school to learn English and Spanish. She was living with another man then, but he treated me well. The house was surrounded by plantains and the children ate bananas every morning. The men rowed out in their boats to catch the shrimps: the big catch in March lasts only three days, when the shrimps come in to the river mouth. Then the men wake up at one in the morning to start fishing, because by May the rains have come and they're gone for another year. We'd dry the shrimps and if I sold a catch I'd walk to Port and with the savings buy flour, sugar and beans. Then I'd make pancakes and sweet bread, which sold really well. In those days friends would bring up the river by canoe the things that you needed from Port, like tools or petrol. After a hunt in the hills the families would all take a share of the meat, but now if you hear there's some pork you need money. No money, no nothing. And these days it's too dangerous to plant out in the bush. We stay at home in Wawa. Only the strong and brave plant their rice, they then harvest and dry it, pound it and let the wind blow away the dust. Then they have their rice and can eat.

My mother fell very ill when I was twelve and went to the Bilwaskarma hospital, but she only became worse, so my aunt brought her home to die. My aunt then became my new mother. When I was fourteen I had to work as a child-minder and cleaner for a Chinese family in Port and was paid five *cordobas* a month, enough to buy myself a suit and underwear. Then an American lady stopped me in Port and asked me, 'Why don't you come and work for me? I'll pay you ten *cordobas* a month. Just tell your boss your mother's sick and you have to visit her.' I felt nervous telling Mrs Chepita this story, but that's how I left and – boom, boom – there I was in this new house of the gringa, and only doing baby-minding. And again it wasn't long before another lady, Mrs Evans, offered me fifteen *cordobas*, so up I got and left the American.

I was fifteen when my aunt wanted me back and sent me to school again. I'd missed a lot of schooling but was quite smart because I passed all my exams well. But in the third grade my aunt hit bad times and we had to move to Port to grow vegetables. She had eight children and couldn't afford to buy our clothes. Her drunken husband wasn't much help either.

I started work in a hairdresser's in Port when I became a woman, at sixteen. There a man fell in love with me. At first I felt frightened, and I didn't want him; but you know how men are, talking, talking, and eventually he won me over.

But after seven years he was driving me mad with his drinking and other women. When I eventually caught him with another woman I told him, 'Either her or me, one or the other, but not the two.' Well, he wanted the other more, so that was that. They went off to Bluefields and I was left with three children. So I started working again and worked really hard. Then I met another man and I had a girl by him; but again after seven years he went off with another woman. 'Well,' I said to myself, 'with the two of them gone, that's enough, no more men.' And since then I've stayed alone.

This was when I became a midwife. It happened like this. When I had my first baby I had this midwife – oh, and what a midwife! There she was smoking away and drinking coffee, while I did all the work. I thought midwives were meant to help, but not this one. It was a miracle I got through alive. I made the decision then and there that when I had my next baby I would know everything I needed to be able to handle my own deliveries alone. And this I did, five times in all. I had everything ready. I took the herbal waters when the pain came on and when the baby was born I cut the umbilical cord myself with clean scissors.

After that first one, word spread straight away that I'd delivered my own baby. The women began saying, 'Helena should be our midwife.' I thought it over carefully – attending to other women's babies was another matter, after all – but I started helping, and thank God there's never been a bad delivery. Then in 1972 the United States funded a midwives' project in Port, and there I learnt some more and almost became a doctor in the communities. In Port a new hospital was built with everything we needed for doing deliveries. Local midwives came in for a week's training and practice. I was asked to take charge of the project, which I did for five years.

But with the 1979 triumph the gringos left and the project ended. And things haven't got any better. Life is too expensive; the people have to raise the price of their produce to be able to buy the imported stuff; the

Miskito Indians return to their communities during the 1985 ceasefire

communities are ruined; women are without their men. We no longer have hens, pigs and cows; only dogs and horses are left, and who wants to eat them? The last battle at home in Wawa was in 1984. Before, many people came to settle because it was so pretty. Now it's all overgrown. Cows kept the grass down, but now you have to use a machete, but you can't sharpen the machete because there's no stone, and anyway there are no machetes. That last battle was a disaster. I fled into the bush with three old ladies, my daughter and her husband and their four children. We walked until I could go no further. I begged to be left behind, but they wouldn't leave me. I was carrying one of the grandchildren and the bags across the swamp and I nearly gave up. 'Dear Lord, help me,' I cried. I couldn't take any more. Then my son-in-law took the child and we reached dry ground. There he made a palm shelter. The fighting eventually quietened. After eight days the food was finished, and I said we had to return. The old ladies were frightened so I said I'd go alone with the children, but obviously it was better if we kept together, so the next day we all set off. Then two helicopters and planes flew over us towards Haulover, and we heard bombing for two days.

When we arrived in Wawa there were militias there to welcome us. 'Why did you stay away for so long?' they asked. We told them we were frightened by the bombing. They said, 'Ah, nothing would have happened to you, we were chasing out the enemy.' Everyone had returned to Wawa, but oh, what a mess! All the houses had been pillaged – everything taken: towels, jackets, sheets, the beds all upside down, with mattresses ripped up. Even the girls' birthday savings had gone.

But I don't wish to speak badly of those Sandinistas in Wawa. They helped us with provisions as we were left with absolutely nothing. We made our claim from the government. I went myself to the office to demand my things, radio, pickaxe, hammer. This happened because of the war, this war made by the Contra, not us.

Doris Gabay

A Creole and a retired headmistress of the Moravian school in Puerto Cabezas. She spoke to us in English.

I'm Doris Gabay of Puerto Cabezas. My father was Jamaican and my mother from the Grand Cayman Islands, and they came to live in Nicaragua when they were children. I was born in 1916 and over the years I've seen so many changes I hardly know where to begin. The teaching system is very different now. For instance all my studies were in English up to sixth grade in elementary school in Bluefields. But my father thought that some of his eight children should know Spanish too, so he sent me to a Catholic school where only Spanish was taught. I had to start right at the bottom in second grade, but I did so well that within a year and a half I completed second, third and fourth grades and went through to seventh, and then the nuns put me to teach. I was nineteen years old and eventually I got to love it very much and spent the rest of my life as a schoolteacher. I've spent nearly sixty years in the classroom. During the 1940s the Nicaraguan government decided to nationalise all schools and teaching in Spanish became compulsory.

In those days the best schools in Bluefields were those belonging to the different church denominations. They were independent and kept up-to-date, the Anglican schools following mainly the English system, the Moravian the American system and the Catholic following the Spanish system. Some of the teachers came from the United States and headteachers from Jamaica. In those days the teaching standard was higher, and the children in sixth grade could actually compose poems and compositions. The main difference now is the curriculum, where there is great emphasis put on physical exercise. When I studied, the first subject of the day was sewing and embroidery for the girls, next was arithmetic, then grammar that covered reading, writing, spelling and composition. We studied the sciences, botany and zoology, and later in sixth grade chemistry and physics were added. Emphasis was put on to mathematics and language. One of the beautiful things that every school enjoyed was contests in spelling and reciting from memory. I still remember a poem I learnt when I was nine. It has quite a history. When England was ruled by a governor, Oliver Cromwell, a young girl did a very, very strange and heroic thing to save her lover who was imprisoned and condemned to die at the tolling of the curfew hour. She climbed the bell tower to stop the bell ringing out:

> *Out she swung, far out,*
> *The city scene was now a speck of light below,*
> *Twixt heaven and earth her arms suspended*
> *As the girl swung to and fro*
> *And the old man at the bell rope*
> *Deaf, heard no bell.*
> *But he thought it still was ringing,*
> *Create young Basil's funeral knell.*
> *But the girl swung most firmly,*
> *And her white lips saying,*
> *Curfew shall not ring tonight.*

Over the distant hills came Cromwell.
Bessy sees him and eyes full of hope
And full of gladness has no anxious trace now.
At his feet she tells her story,
Shows her hands are bruised and sore,
And her face so sweet and tender
And pleading, touched his heart
With such pity filled his eyes with misty light.
'Go your lover lives,' said Cromwell,
'Curfew shall not ring tonight.'

That is a story that really happened. I wonder how a girl of fifteen did such a brave deed to save her lover? I just love that poem.

I began teaching at nineteen and after two whole years I still hadn't married. So I asked my parents' permission to visit Puerto Cabezas for a short holiday – I didn't dare tell them that I wanted to look for a husband. While I was there staying with friends my present husband came to visit the house. He too was looking for a wife. I have a lot of faith in prayers: I believe the Lord brought us together. We kept company for two weeks and before I left he asked for my hand in marriage. And how he asked! 'I wonder what's the price of a wedding dress?' he said. And that was around forty years ago. We made our marriage plans by letter and in March we married in the Moravian Church with bridesmaids and groomsmen. It was quite a wedding, and for two years I stopped teaching. He worked on a hydro-electric plant at the American gold mine which supplied the entire population with electricity. Life was rough. I wasn't accustomed to doing housework, cooking and washing. Then he fell ill with tuberculosis, and in those days there was no sanatorium, so he had to go to Costa Rica for eleven months to be cured, during which time I fell sick too. Because of this we have never been able to have any children. It was difficult. Then, in 1949, I was asked to teach here in the Moravian school, where I stayed until 1982 as headteacher. To make things easier at home we were always able to find a Miskito woman who would do the housework, wash our clothes and cook the food. All of us schoolteachers hired them as maids. The American wives also hired maids, but they were Creole women.

After they finished their schooling, most young men got jobs in the lumber company here. Some girls trained to be nurses at the Bilwaskarma Moravian hospital. The United States helped to fund this work – the first graduate nurse in Nicaragua was from there. Very few students went on to higher education as parents couldn't afford to send their children to Bluefields or Managua.

We called the Pacific side of the country the interior. It belonged to the Spaniards and very few people from the Coast got the chance to go there. It seemed as if whoever was president didn't do much, and certainly didn't interest themselves in the progress of the Coast. I remember Father grumbling about the fact that all our taxes went to Managua and nothing came back. There were always good relations between the government and the American companies. They received concessions and not much was asked in return. They were here for years taking out gold and timber, so they ought to have built this place up. Now their houses have fallen into decay, they're the shabbiest ones here, and because of the war there's no timber for us to do the repairs.

The ships used to come in every week to take out the lumber and deliver stuff for the stores. You could buy anything if you had the money, or buy in instalments. Now we have to buy according to how the government has organised distribution in the neighbourhood stores, where we buy only a certain amount according to the size of our family. We can't find some things like butter, yeast and yellow cheese. Once we could buy imported raisins, currants, apples and grapes. But, bless the Lord, we are provided for. We're not going to starve, because we have the sea and we can fish down at the beach, and we have lots of fruit trees. Now we are enjoying oranges in our yard and the bananas and breadfruit and coconuts are growing.

In Puerto Cabezas there used to be two clubs, one Spanish, the other Creole, and there were parties there every week. We still have a picture house, which has been here for over fifty years, and the churches put on plays which have come from the States, either dramas or comedies, which everyone loves. The last play we had was to raise money for the poor, and outside on the porch there were sales of ice cream and cakes. Along with the national celebration of the Sandinista victory every 19 July, here the Battle of San Jacinto is celebrated as an important day. This is because in 1856 an American came to Nicaragua, a filibuster called William Walker,[1] and little by little he took over the country. Costa Rica joined Nicaragua in trying to get him out, but it wasn't until the decisive Battle of San Jacinto, when a handful of Nicaraguans attacked him, that the man was finally thrown out.

I don't think the United States blockade against Nicaragua has been done deliberately to hurt the people

Things are getting worse, like I was telling my friends: 'Look, last month, we should be catching shrimps and fish and we not catching none, whole month none. So right there we must know that the Lord got for us lots of changes coming.'
Bonnie Margaret Moore, a Creole market woman in Puerto Cabezas

Bonnie's children play on sea cargo destroyed by the Contra

here. I think it's because the Americans believe that communism is entering this part of the world. But we're not so sure ourselves that this is the case. When we look around we see some improvements, new things that the government has started. There used not to be so much work in this town; now lots of people are busy working in construction and many girls are studying to be secretaries so that they can get jobs in the new offices. On the other hand, about 50 per cent of the men are in uniform, fighting a war, and lots of people have left for the United States where the standard of living is much higher. Others have gone because they don't like the government.

As for me, these days my chief interest is studying the Bible, because I believe that there lie all the answers to life's problems. It is the one guide, and if all government leaders followed it the world would be different: the Lord would come quickly and everything would be better.

[1]One of the most eccentric efforts at US domination often recalled by Nicaraguans was the arrival in 1856 of a Tennessee slave owner and adventurer, William Walker. Initially he came with US backing to aid the Liberals, but he proclaimed himself president, using Nicaraguan territory as collateral to obtain foreign loans, and reinstated slavery, confiscated Nicaraguan landholdings for redistribution to US citizens and declared English as the official language. This audacity was too much for Nicaragua and its neighbours, and he lasted only two years in power.

Puerto Cabezas Moravian church

Andy Shogreen

A Creole minister and head of the Moravian Church. He spoke to us in English.

The Moravian Church came about because of a split in the Catholic Church during the fifteenth century in what today we call Czechoslovakia. The repression forced its followers into exile to Prussia, where the church grew and began its overseas missionary work.

When the church arrived on the Atlantic Coast of Nicaragua in the nineteenth century this region was held by the English Protectorate. At that time Miskito kings were permitted to govern the whole of the Atlantic Coast region which extended into Honduras and Costa Rica. One Miskito king presented some land to the Prince of Prussia who then got it surveyed. The survey showed that the Miskito people had very little education, were very superstitious and very immoral. It was their immorality in particular which motivated the Prince of Prussia to recommend our church to begin missionary work here.

The Miskitos did have a God but it wasn't clear what he represented, and this Miskito king, though not a Christian himself, welcomed the missionary work. On 14 March 1849, this work began with an open-air service in Bluefields. From there missionaries spread out to Pearl Lagoon, Tasbapauni and up to the north. By the time the church reached Puerto Cabezas around 1925 the majority of the Miskito communities had been evangelised.

More recently other churches have appeared, to 'steal the sheep' as they say. But the Moravian Church, under our motto of 'Unity', is the main church here: its philosophy and the feelings of the indigenous people are at one. The church believes in the values of simplicity and in the true practice of Christian living. It is concerned not only for the soul of man but for his health and intellectual and economic development. The missionaries began by building schools, providing a health service, and teaching the communities to plant coconut palms and other fruit trees. Drunkenness was common so the missionaries stressed self-control in moral conduct and tried to instil a sense of the consecrated Christ-like way of life. You don't find police or jail-houses in the indigenous communities and there is rarely any violence here. Of course it has always been a quite peaceful place, but I consider the missionary work has strengthened these values.

The church effectively became the regional government,

I don't see what good going to happen in Nicaragua, because preacher was telling us the Bible say that these other non-believers will come and kill. That's why he preaching to make these people have faith in God. The preacher say, 'God forgive them, because they know not what they are doing. They take what coming to them later on,' he say, 'that hell happen to them.'
Bonnie Margaret Moore, a Creole market women in Puerto Cabezas

even during the times of the English Protectorate. England and consequent governments were more interested in exploiting the natural resources while the church gained the people's recognition and respect for bringing them education and health care and for translating the Bible into Miskito. The people belong to our church.

The Catholic Church never took root here. The Spanish conquerors met with strong resistance from the Indian people and this effectively kept the two sides of the country separate. The Indians here consider the Pacific people their enemy, and with reason, given how the Spanish treated the Indians on their side of the country. Most have disappeared or have been absorbed into the Spanish culture, while here the strong Indian way of life still survives. In part this enmity stems also from the English and Spanish colonial rivalry. Still to this day the Pacific Mestizos don't understand the Indians' culture and many Miskitos don't speak Spanish, making communication hard. The Mestizos' insistence on their right to govern the Indians has also caused problems. The church has tried to build bridges between the people and the government, to bring peace and understanding.

When Nicaragua became independent from Spain and the Managuan government laid claim to the Atlantic Coast, the people couldn't see why their lives should be changed. In our registry books dating back to before the incorporation of the Atlantic Coast, people registered their babies' nationality as Miskito. The incorporation caused great resentment and revolts took place in an attempt to re-establish a Miskito kingdom, similar to the famous one in Yulú, which was led by a Moravian pastor.

When the struggle of Sandino happened I don't think the people here understood what it was about, because their interests were always different. Sandino was interested in the defence of Nicaraguan sovereignty which was not the preoccupation here. The Indians don't see Nicaragua as a country. They see their country as their community and their territory as the Atlantic Coast.

Alta Hooker

A Creole nurse living in Puerto Cabezas. She is the mother of two children.

Before the revolution I was working as a nurse at the hospital in Puerto Cabezas. Although I hadn't been trained in anaesthetics, I was put in charge of this work.

Then, following the triumph, there were some tremendous changes. We found ourselves faced with problems we'd never tackled before. The Sandinistas began socialising the health service, and we were told that everyone now had the right to receive free medical care and that the hospital staff would start going out to the surrounding communities to improve health conditions there. Well, frankly, to many this made no sense at all. There simply weren't enough nurses to handle the entire population. And the hospital only had twenty-five beds, so when people began arriving from all over they had to sleep on the floor. But we managed to cope all right.

Then in 1980 I went to Managua to study anaesthetics. The course was in Spanish, and as I normally speak English I found it quite tough going. And the other students were very different from me. It really shocked me when they asked if they needed passports to visit the Atlantic Coast and if we wore native costumes. They even asked why we wanted to live there! They knew next to nothing about the Atlantic Coast. It's true, of course, that we think differently and have our own languages – but we're still Nicaraguan.

When I returned to Puerto Cabezas there'd been a lot more changes. The hospital workers had unionised and the people had a much better idea of what was going on. But I didn't join the union. Like many Creoles I was pretty narrow-minded and conformist at the time. We like to live life as we choose. We'll go to church, to work, come home, but organise anything other than a party – no way.

But then I became friends with a doctor. He was the one who explained what the revolution was all about – that it was the opportunity for everyone to advance and to contribute to making life better. But it was when we went to work in the countryside that my way of thinking really began to change. There I met Sandinista soldiers who were making a real personal sacrifice to protect the people of Puerto Cabezas. These young men and women were sleeping rough, eating badly, were often sick because they'd get soaking wet; and they were all covered with flea and mosquito bites. This had a big impact on me – I'd

never really put myself out for anybody, except maybe for my family.

But my husband didn't go along with this. For him it wasn't important to improve the lives of others, especially if you weren't getting paid for it. And he complained that I wasn't spending enough time at home. We nearly reached the point of divorce.

I'm much clearer now about what's happened here on the Atlantic Coast. You see, the root of the problem in this region is that people here are divided by what I call class racism. We Creoles have always considered ourselves more intelligent than any of the indigenous peoples like the

Miskitos recently returned to their community during the 1985 ceasefire

Miskito Indians or the Sumus or the Ramas who live out in the bush. But the Mestizos, who are descendants of the Spanish and come from the Pacific side of the country, think themselves superior to everyone. When the English first colonised this area in the seventeenth century, they brought the Creoles from the Caribbean to work for them. They also used the Miskito Indians as guerrillas to hold back the Spaniards on the Pacific Coast. So, when the 'Spanish' – that is, Mestizo – revolutionaries arrived here after the triumph, they were not seen as brothers, more like conquistadors who'd come to govern us. The CIA took great advantage of the tensions that already existed between the various ethnic groups and, in the end, handled the situation much more skilfully than those who had made the revolution possible.

The CIA focused their attention on the majority group in North Zelaya, the Miskitos, because of their deep-rooted distrust of the Mestizos. Indirectly the CIA managed to organise them into an armed force to fight against the revolutionary government. And how did the CIA do this? Through Steadman Fagoth, one of MISURASATA's leaders.

At that time he was a very popular leader amongst the Miskitos. When the Literacy Crusade started in 1980 the Sandinista government decided after some hesitation that the indigenous people should be taught in their own language. Steadman organised his MISURASATA literacy teachers to use this opportunity to campaign for the separation of the Atlantic Coast which caused the Sandinistas great alarm. This work also served to convince the Miskitos that the Sandinista, the 'Spanish', never would answer their demands, that they never were and never would be their brothers, but always colonialists. The situation deteriorated very quickly, and as you know the CIA isn't slow. Miskito men left for Honduras and Costa Rica to be organised into armed forces to destabilise the new government. The CIA supplied everything to build racial hostility into war.

Mildred Levy

A Creole midwife, now retired and living in Puerto Cabezas.

In the Miskito communities it's the women who keep Miskito traditions alive. They do most of the plantation work – the men only fell the trees. It's important that a woman has children so that they can help do the work. The woman has to obey her man and doesn't take any big decisions as she is considered a lesser person. Yet when the men go to work, as they did to the gold mines, the women are left with most of the farming. He returns when the land's ready for sowing again.

The Miskitos work in a collective way, doing their turtling for a certain time, then the farming, and while the crops are growing they'll go hunting. Likewise when the shrimps come into the lagoons for a few months the men go and catch them before they return to the sea. So they call the months by animal names – the terrapin, then the iguana – and that animal is only hunted during its named month. In this way there's time for nature to be replenished.

Their medicines are made from roots and vines and are boiled or pounded. They can cure fevers, kidney complaints and snake bites. Interestingly, this government is looking into these old medicines, especially since the US blockade, but only a few know how to use them. These medicine men also can calm psychological upsets. The Miskitos are very superstitious and often believe they're ill because they've been cursed, and they'll say, 'This isn't for the hospital, this is for our medicine man.'

Of course Christianity has had a big influence amongst the Miskitos but many of them still believe in the King of the Bush and say that if you lose your way in the jungle then the little Bush King came and stole you, and if you drown they'll say the Worm King pulled you under his waters. And the moon holds great importance, determining many aspects of their lives.

We began work with the local Miskito midwives way back in 1972. They came to Puerto Cabezas to attend courses we'd organised. They had their own way of doing their deliveries – the traditional delivery position is generally a sitting one and today the medical world is coming round to accept that as the natural way – but their handling of the umbilical cord often caused infections. Following training this improved and the death rate dropped. With this work I felt closer to the people. Then in 1973 the indigenous organisation, ALPROMISU, was born and we began working with communities throughout the region – I was responsible for finance: I felt I should do more than my eight-hour nursing job. In the communities we had discussions with the people and carried out fund-raising activities. Representatives from 100 communities came to the first General Assembly in Sinsin in 1974. We wanted the people to have access to further education, so that they could return to teach their own people, and that there should be price controls on their fish and timber because in those days the American companies decided the prices. We also wanted land rights, especially for the River Coco people who, though having lived there for hundreds of years, had no legal claim to their lands.

ALPROMISU didn't go deeply into issues such as rights over the gold found in this region. This only started when MISURASATA was established in 1979 and met with other indigenous peoples at the first World Indigenous Conference where rights over natural resources were discussed. We had new leaders from university, boys and girls like Hazel Lau, Steadman Fagoth and Brooklyn Rivera. Before that, friends like Miss Hert who'd no university training helped run the organisation. So we went along with these new leaders, thinking this was best for the people. Now we know that some of these people had very different aspirations, and maybe today's conflict stems from then.

When this government came to power, they consulted the leaders of MISURASATA over all the health-service planning in the region, so that together they could work out the best places to establish health centres. The government didn't step in without consultation. In Francia Sirpi we were hoping to have a maternity clinic beside the agricultural coco plant with a team of a doctor and nurses. But it remains empty. None of this work can continue; it's all up in the air because of the fighting.

After the 1979 triumph there were such improvements in health care. We managed to get measles under control; we delivered vaccines to refrigerated depots throughout the region and from there the native health leaders would pick them up in thermos boxes and go and vaccinate their people. And where is all this today? How can the people receive the medical attention they need when it's so risky to go out there? The people keep coming from the communities saying, 'We have so many sick children.' But what can we do?

Hazel Lau

A Miskito woman, a founder leader of MISURASATA and an elected FSLN candidate to the National Assembly from North Zelaya.

Centuries ago the Miskitos displaced the Sumu Indians from their lands along the River Coco. In their search for security the Sumus have remained isolated and have kept their traditions and physiology while the Miskitos have married into other ethnic groups and adopted foreign and Christian values. The Sumus call them Miskitonaya – *naya* means 'divided'.

Before the colonial era, before 1521, the Miskitos lived under chieftains. Their priests, the *sukia*, were also medicine men; they interwove religion and healing and held positions of great authority. The Moravian Church exerted great influence over the Miskitos, and the *sukia* Indian priests became Moravian pastors, which helped keep alive certain Miskito beliefs within the church. For instance, the week after a Moravian funeral the Miskitos will dance a ritual to free the spirit. They still believe they must die where their umbilical cord is buried, where they were born, so as to return to the earth where they belong. This explains the great importance the Miskitos placed on their return from the Tasba Pri settlement to their River Coco communities.

The historical divide between the Pacific and Atlantic Coasts really began during the colonial era when the Spanish were faced with fierce Indian resistance. It was the English who moved in, supplying the Miskitos with muskets to fuel their resistance against the Spanish and conveniently allowing for England's commercial interests in the Atlantic Coast to continue uninterrupted for two centuries. When England and Spain signed the Treaty of Managua in 1860, this supposedly gave the Atlantic Coast people autonomy. But with the English removed, the United States was ready to take over, providing military backing for Zelaya's Nicaraguan government to reincorporate the Atlantic Coast in 1894. Nicaragua repaid the US handsomely. American companies plundered the region's natural resources of wood, fruit and gold so that the Atlantic Coast became a US enclave. The Americans established towns like Puerto Cabezas with company stores overflowing with US products. It was a world apart from the Pacific side and there was little or no contact until the Second World War when a foreign air company started daily flights.

By the 1960s only the mining companies remained. Nicaragua had been the world's second largest gold exporter to the United States. But you can bet the people weren't taught to question why the place remained impoverished. Some Creoles even romanticise about those 'good old days'.

In the 1960s the Miskito way of life began to be seriously threatened when new boundaries were drawn up between Nicaragua and Honduras. Miskito lands were signed over to Honduras. Tension grew and in 1970 the Honduran military attacked a Miskito community. It was a bloodbath. Then Somoza's nationalisation of lands around Puerto Cabezas prohibited communities from felling their trees. The Sumus near the mining area were designated lands they didn't want. Tired of the National Guard's repression and government officials, the Sumus responded with machetes. All this helped to bring the Sumus and Miskitos together to set up ALPROMISU in 1976. Their aims were to reclaim the lands designated to them in the 1860 treaty, and reinstate teaching in the indigenous languages. But Somoza wasn't going to let Nicaragua's most marginalised groups get organised, and true to style he brought pressure to bear and the organisation's leadership bowed down.

But in 1977 things began to change when Brooklyn Rivera, Alfonso Smith, Steadman Fagoth and myself got involved in ALPROMISU. At the time we were all studying at university in Managua. In the growing chaos of 1978 the university was hardly functioning, so we used the recessions to go home and help in the running of the organisation. With the '79 triumph the old ALPROMISU president fled, fearing imprisonment, and we were asked to take over the leadership. The people held great hopes for the Sandinista revolution, believing this would answer all their demands. But it wasn't long before trouble began when the old Somoza administrators, looking for ways to placate the FSLN, began intrigues against ALPROMISU, hoping to draw suspicion away from them and on to us. And it worked. Several ALPROMISU members were imprisoned, but they were soon released after we protested their innocence.

In November that year at our fifth assembly ALPROMISU was renamed MISURASATA and we launched our 1980 plan. One of our main tasks was to co-ordinate the Literacy Crusade in the different ethnic languages and to make claims for the communities' land titles. This involved doing a land survey which was placed in Fagoth's hands.

We also drew up an agreement with the National Forestry Board in which they were to pay 80 per cent of the wood value back to the communities. They failed to comply, and using this, Fagoth took it upon himself to bring Puerto Cabezas to a standstill. All transport came to a halt and all the shops closed, even as far away as Waspan on the River Coco. Brooklyn was at the mines and I in Waspan starting the Literacy Crusade when rumours reached us that Fagoth was in prison and going to be killed. I decided to go and talk with government officials, but it seemed they were unable to handle the situation. To break the deadlock it was agreed that the MISURASATA leadership should meet officially with government representatives. Fagoth refused to come, saying he had to visit the River Coco. This left Brooklyn and me to dampen down the flames that Fagoth had started. When the MISURASATA leadership met in December 1980 I told Brooklyn that the people had a right to know that it was Fagoth who had made the government distrustful of the organisation, since it was the people who would suffer for it. But Fagoth had begged Brooklyn for his support, saying 'The people will never forgive me, I'll never do this again,' and Brooklyn asked me not to denounce Fagoth in public.

Then in 1981 was the next real breakdown in relationships with the FSLN. The US State Department had begun to fund and train the Somoza National Guard and by January 1981 Contra activity was growing. The Sandinistas responded by declaring a state of emergency, banning outdoor public meetings. Fagoth, fully aware of this, organised a meeting of MISURASATA literacy teachers, deliberately provoking the Sandinistas to jail them. I told Brooklyn things had gone too far. Because of this the authorities had lost all trust in us. To try and clear up the situation I asked for a meeting with the national leadership and told Fagoth he'd have to attend, to which he replied, 'I've explained everything to Brooklyn. You and he can take care of things. I have to go to Honduras to see my uncle.' He knew he'd pushed his luck too far. The FSLN leadership were aware that he'd been a member of Somoza's State Security, but had accepted him because of his popularity in the Coast.

Further concern was caused by the 1981 MISURASATA plan in which Fagoth demanded to be part of the national leadership and the land claim far exceeded government expectations and appeared to be a claim for Miskito independence from Nicaragua. Before Fagoth could escape we were all arrested and accused of acts against the State of Emergency. MISURASATA leaders were arrested from Bluefields, Bonanza, Rosita, Puerto Cabezas and Waspan. Straight away the Atlantic Coast people rose up in indignation. Thousands gathered in the churches to demand our release. This was given after fourteen days and all charges were dropped. Two peace commissions sprang up, one under MISURASATA, the other loyal to Fagoth. Fagoth was the only remaining prisoner and pressure for his release continued. People were unwilling to believe he'd been part of Somoza's State Security.

In April 1981 a group of Fagoth's men went over to Honduras and threatened armed action, pressing for his release. Meanwhile MISURASATA continued to negotiate for his freedom, which we achieved on 6 May, with the proviso that he went and stayed abroad. Fagoth's response to this was to disappear six days later. He crossed the River Coco where he was met by a Honduran captain and trucks full of soldiers. Two days later Fagoth declared war on the Sandinistas over the Contra radio station, calling on Miskito men to come and follow him. MISURASATA countered this, calling on our people to return from Honduras, which some of the men did.

The FSLN were wiser in their dealings with MISURASATA, but feeling the pressure from the US they demanded to know where we stood. We stated that we supported the revolutionary process, but within the context of pursuing indigenous interests. We knew the Indian struggle wouldn't be furthered by Fagoth's armed faction, MISURA, fighting along with Somoza National Guard whose interests totally differed from the Indian people's. Even so, tension existed with the government, and a number of MISURASATA people went over to the other side, including Brooklyn. He told me he'd felt his time was up, that his life was in danger.

Brooklyn signed an agreement with another Contra group, Pastora's ARDE. I wrote to Brooklyn telling him that there was no guarantee that this organisation would fight for Indian interests. For me the agreement that he'd signed – that Miskito, Sumu, Rama Indians and Creoles have the right to their ethnic development – was completely ambiguous. I told him ARDE was out to use him and his men, and that they'd succeed. Brooklyn said he was willing to talk with the government and I set about arranging this. By now the people wanted a peace settlement negotiated. They had been overwhelmed by how fast the situation had deteriorated, with their communities destroyed, families broken up or displaced to new settlements in Tasba Pri.

It was the women's persistent demands on the government that allowed the Miskito people to return to their old communities. The new representative in Puerto Cabezas, Sub-Commander José Gonzales of the Ministry of the Interior, was particularly receptive and after one year of talks it was decided that the homeward journey could begin, and that once the military situation permitted, the people could return to the River Coco. This became a reality with the 1985 ceasefire between MISURA and the army.

The women hold the communities together and through these troubled years have shown themselves to be stronger than their men. But the political Indian movements ignore them and women hardly have a presence in the autonomy project. I've pointed this out to them, saying 'When you men were imprisoned it was the women who fought for your release, faced every situation, so where are these women today?'

The ruined Waspan church. Following the 1982 evacuation of the River Coco peoples, their communities were destroyed to prevent their use by rebel forces

The people are divided between civilian and armed groups. There's not one organisation that represents the Atlantic Coast people. But the people are starting to see their way out of this conflict through the autonomy process. Naturally it means different things to different people, but everyone's main concern at the moment is peace.

The racial-class divisions created by our troubled history left animosities that cannot disappear overnight. But autonomy is the means to learn how to live together, and is the formula for peace. A regional government will unite all sectors as the people gain their rights. This would foil the United States in its policy of divide and rule. The people are so tired of the war and long to sleep in peace with their families united. There no longer exists a social base to support this war.

Verónica Gonzales

A Mestizo woman who moved with her husband from Jinotega when he began work with the Forestry Board on the Atlantic Coast. They now live in Puerto Cabezas.

We were in bed when the attack happened. It was 22 April 1983. It was late, around ten; the generator was switched off in Slimalila; the shooting started. We thought it must be the Sandinista *compas* fighting back MISURA. We stayed quietly in bed, waiting to see what would happen. But we only heard the shouting of MISURA slogans in Miskito and the Miskito people supporting them, calling back. We remained silent. Then the rebels came to the house, swearing, 'You Spanish bastards!' They threatened to throw a bomb into the house if we didn't come out. As we stepped into the road they fired bullets all around our feet. We were ordered to walk to Yunate. It was a march through swamplands. At Yunate we rested and they told us our destination was Honduras. My heart sank. I was three months pregnant and our small son was with us. There were around 1,800 of us and there were about 450 MISURA men. They left their own kind alone, but as we weren't Miskito they treated us badly, humiliating us.

When some planes flew over, searching for people who'd been kidnapped, we were pushed into the river and kept at gunpoint. There a woman started labour pains and had her baby. After five minutes she was forced to move on. We had no water or food, so I asked MISURA for some crackers for my child, and for this they said that if I complained again they'd slit my throat. Eventually we arrived at the River Coco. There another woman had her baby. They took us across in their canoes and from there we passed through some MISURA Contra camps, until we stopped in one near Mocorón, where we were interrogated. They said they were fighting to save the Miskito people. I told them, 'I need no saving, only from what's happening to me now.' There were hundreds of people in the camp. In others I'd seen women as well, some of them are fighters.

We queued there for some beans, but they were all gone well before we'd reached the end, so again we slept on empty stomachs. We'd hardly eaten in a week, and the children were starving. The MISURA ordered the men to leave their women and march to Rus Rus military base for training, to prepare them to fight against Nicaragua. My husband refused to go. He said he wouldn't fight for a cause he didn't believe in, so we were put to one side with six others and taken to the Mocorón refugee centre. In the United Nations refugee office we told the gringos we originated from Jinotega before moving to work in the forestry office in Slimalila. They gave us some food and to the MISURA men as well.

We were put into a refugee camp but conditions were so bad my husband found work in Mocorón on a farm. There we earned enought to eat, and the farm wife gave me a dress, as mine was in tatters. He did building, soldering and unloading boats while I did washing. The hut we lived in was full of fleas and the rain poured through the palm roof, though we tried patching it up with tin. After six months we found work on a farm near to the River Coco, from where we hoped to escape back to Nicaragua.

The day came when the owner left for Mocorón and we decided to make our escape. At three in the morning we took their canoe out across the River Coco to the Nicaraguan side. I can't describe how we felt: we wanted to cry, weep for joy, but we were terrified too. I told my boy to keep quiet as we'd be killed if caught.

We lost our way in the mountains since there were no paths. Suddenly there was an outbreak of shooting. We were sure it was MISURA. We froze, terrified. We hid there till dawn, before setting off again. It was very hard going. I was about to give birth, we had no shoes and we were very hungry, though we did find some bananas. After five days we reached Leimos Nicaragua. It used to be a Miskito community but the people had gone to the Tasba Pri settlement. There was plenty of fruit growing so we ate until a big storm broke, soaking us through. My poor boy trembled with cold.

From there we walked on until we saw a watch tower. I took out a white sheet and tied it to a stick, and walked with it above my head for the Sandinista *compas* in the tower to see. They came down to us. We felt such relief. We told them everything that had happened and showed our Sandino coins we'd kept hidden, to prove we were Nicaraguan. We were taken to their building where the child ate, and a military chief arrived to question us. We had a huge meal there, we stuffed ourselves. Then my labour pains started and a doctor came and put me on an intravenous drip until a plane arrived and took me to Port. It all worked out well in the end, I had a girl. We were so happy.

It was like a dream to be back amongst friends and see the sea again.

MISURA really deceive the refugee organisations. They tell them that people like us have fled from Sandinista aggression, when it's MISURA who've attacked us. But the authorities must believe them because MISURA receive help in Honduras where they have their military bases. They're building a lot of roads around Mocorón. We saw planes and helicopters arriving to deliver arms and supplies to the Rus Rus base. The gringo refugee workers don't realise that the people are kidnapped. They're all refugees to them.

Now lots of Miskitos want to return to their families, but MISURA tell them the Sandinistas will cut off their tongues and they'll be imprisoned for thirty years. But the Sandinistas want peace and all those who have returned, including the fighters, have received pardon under the amnesty, and you see them freely walking around Port.

THE PACIFIC COAST

THROWING A LIFELINE

Rita López

An Indian woman living in the mountain village of El Chile in the Matagalpa region.

Today Pastor Mendoza owns all the land. He stole from Felicito Garcia after paying some men twenty *pesos* each to knife to death Garcia, his pregnant woman and their four children. They worked all night to bury the bodies.

Pastor Mendoza murdered for land.

Now we don't have any good land. We heard the Agrarian Reform Ministry had bought us some but they hadn't, so our men from the co-operative went and sowed on forty acres of Pastor Mendoza's land. The Pastor just ran his cattle through to destroy our harvest.

We get by on a few beans and rice that the Agrarian Reform Ministry gives us. We only have two acres that we rent from Santos Moñoz.

Not long ago Pastor Mendoza called on my son and told him and the men to stop making trouble. They're demanding back 300 acres for the community. The land

Rita López walks back home

Children cut the palm leaf to wrap up maize cakes

we have now is useless – scrub for cattle. You can't plant on it.[1]

Thirty years ago Pastor threw me and the children out on to the street. He sold my home when it wasn't even his. I was a fool. There we were until a man from here, Francisco Gonzales, took pity on us and sold us a hut. At times I wanted to leave but I couldn't find another village to go to. I went on grinding maize to get by.

There was another landowner like Pastor Mendoza – Captain Rafael Torres. I remember him asking me, 'Do you always want to be miserable when you could be strong, when you could vote for Somoza?' I told him I would never do that, not dead or alive. Father had been a Conservative, and never supported Somoza.

My father went to fight against Santos Zelaya.[2] I remember crying and Father saying, 'Hush now, I'll live if God so wishes. I must go to defend my country.' He fought for three years for Emiliano Chamorro who, when he became President, gave Father thirty acres. Later Father became mayor of the village. Other governments followed and the rich took everything. There was nothing left for the poor; the governments were the owners.

Rita weaving

My mother had fourteen children, but only five of us girls survived. The others died from illness. Father put us to work, pounding rice and beans, just like the men. We used to wake at dawn to work on the land, returning home at three in the afternoon with firewood to cook dinner and do the housework. We never wasted any time. We made pots. Mother said, 'If you marry a man who gives you nothing, how are you going to cook unless you know how to make pots?' We ground coffee and corn, and unravelled yarn as Mother spun. We wove until eleven at night and then slept for three hours. Today women only cook and eat; they're surprised how hard it was.

We never sold our woven cloth. We made it into trousers and skirts to wear ourselves. We used dyes from plants: yellow, coffee, black and blue threads were woven in stripes and animal patterns into a plain background. The cloth I wove was long and fine, red and yellow. In January we picked sackfuls of cotton and by May the harvest was over, ready for planting again. Year after year we sowed. Now it's all gone, the golden cotton we grew.

When Somoza came to power we were told that if the National Guard found us weaving we'd be given a beating.

They took our spindles, threads, looms, everything. They burnt down the cotton fields. They burnt our weavings. They threw them into the flames. There was nothing but smoke. All was ashes.

They came and threw us off our land, so we couldn't work. We ran to the mountains – all this because we didn't support Somoza. Land was given for people's votes. He wanted to buy our free will. Somoza was the only man, the man who ruled the world, the only one.

The old priest, Francisco Payan, used to preach: 'God made the Earth with his hands for us people to go and live where we choose.' Father told us that before we were free to work the land as far as the eye could see. The only use for fences was to protect the vegetables. Grandmother had plenty of land and cows in those days. She grew corn and beans, everything. We all had enough. When a courting couple married we'd kill a cow. There'd be *chicha*, cocoa, bowls full to the brim with food and drink, and we'd dance for two days and nights.

Father didn't like us girls to be near other men. If a man followed me I'd run away, because if Father ever caught a man with me he'd give me a beating. Even Grandmother

Preparing the fire and grinding the corn

Rita feeding the turkeys and hens

warned me, 'You'll be cheated by some man. He'll leave you with a baby in arms.' But I didn't listen to her. I went with a man when I was thirteen, and that was that. But he treated me well, like a daughter. Father was furious. He came to the house after five days; he walked in without permission and hit me. 'Be grateful you're not outside or I'd kill you and send you to the grave,' he said. My father didn't like this man.

I had ten children in all, but was left with only two boys and two girls. The others died as babies, from diarrhoea, temperatures, fevers. It's as though I wasn't meant to have a family. The boys should have lived because boys come out strong. When I was a girl only boys went to school. I wasn't intelligent. I had my conscience, though, and knew that decisions came from God. I had my faith in God. Girls are born to do the work, but I'm ill now, trying to recover from tuberculosis. I shake when I go down to the river to fetch water, I have to rest on the way. It's frightening. It's better I don't go, but the boys don't help me. Still, the youngest won't abandon me.

When Father died from diarrhoea he was still young, and Mother died young as well, from fever.

Rita López's son writes a letter to the Agrarian Reform Ministry requesting that land be given to their community

Today the weaving is being revived. Four of us women are teaching the younger girls to make cloth. There's going to be a cultural house built here, where we'll weave and sell the clothes. We've heard that people from other parts of the world will come to see us and learn.

When I'm well I can weave for about two or three hours and then I have my other chores to do. Don Marcos Altamirano from the local government is the man in charge. He brings the cotton from León, and takes two pieces of cloth every month for a little money. If it wasn't for men working the land we'd all starve.

[1]Since this interview the community of El Chile has received the land it demanded from the Agrarian Reform Ministry.

[2]Thirty-six years of Conservative rule was curtailed by a Liberal revolt in 1893. Their leader, José Santos Zelaya, held presidency for sixteen years and radically modernised Nicaragua. When these national interests became untenable for the United States, and in keeping to the Monroe Doctrine, the US sent in the Marines to back the 1909 Conservative overthrow of Zelaya. Emiliano Chamorro, one of the Conservative leaders, later became president and gave the US exclusive rights in perpetuity to construct a canal on Nicaraguan territory. Although the Conservative landowning class were in part responsible for the indigenous land clearances, in the case of Emiliano Chamorro he repaid his debt to his peasant supporters by giving lands.

One of the few village women who still knows how to do the traditional weaving

An Indian woman making clay pots

Inside one of the El Chile homes

Rita spinning inside her house

MOTHER AND SON

Lesbia Joya Diaz

A mother of nine children, including Wilfredo Joya (q.v.). She works as a cook in the Somoto hospital, Madriz.

I don't see any point in talking about my married life. Why tell you about such misery?

When I separated from my husband I began work in the Tip-Top restaurant. Then I moved to the Somoto hospital to work as a cleaner. The administration knew I had nine children so they kindly gave me better-paid work as a cook. Once in a while Wilfredo's father gives us some beans and corn from his farm, but this year he's provided nothing. He doesn't care. Despite being a woman I've managed to raise the children alone. The wages are just enough to pay for their food, and at times I have to go hungry. I do hope they'll study and do something special with their lives.

All six boys see it as their duty to defend the country. Of course I'd rather Wilfredo was here than in the mountains, but I understand we have to defend Nicaragua. I felt terrible when he was mobilised, but I've come to accept the situation. I still worry if he's away for a long time, but when he tells me where he's going I always try to take him clean clothes and cigarettes. The boys need their mothers. We worry, but we're proud our sons are fighting against such wrong. Perhaps one day we won't suffer as we do now, and everything will change for the better.

Lesbia Joya Diaz visits her son at his military base

Wilfredo Joya Diaz

A twenty-year-old son of Lesbia Joya Diaz (q.v.) and a Sandinista activist, currently serving as educational officer in his battalion.

Father left his lands when I was a boy. He'd had some bad harvests so decided to work for the Somoza police force, which meant we all had to move to Managua. There I got through my primary exams, but because of the '79 insurrection I couldn't finish my secondary education. We were stuck there right through all the fighting. Prices shot up because of the food scarcity and people began looting – they even pillaged factories and banks. We looted a sugar factory – that's when my brother's friend broke his foot when one of the bags fell on it! We had some good laughs, even with the National Guard out to get the likes of us. They murdered thousands of young people; that's why the Sandinistas had such support. It got everyone involved – hiding arms, supplying medicines and food, building barricades. It was the morning of 17 July when I heard Somoza had run off to Miami, and two days later the Sandinistas marched into Managua. They were exhausted and starving, but everyone was *so* happy.

The first thing that was done was to try to bring back

Wilfredo Joya Diaz

civil order and the people began handing over the stolen goods to the FSLN for redistribution to those in greater need. Not surprisingly, Dad was nervous and reckoned he wouldn't find work because of his connection with the Somoza regime. So a few days after the triumph he took off to his lands in Somoto and Mum found work as a cleaner there. The Sandinistas soon came and took Dad in for investigation but he was released after six days. Everyone with ties to Somoza had to be checked through, and some were put inside.

We were very hard up so I went to help out on the land while my brothers and sister stayed on at school. Then in August 1980 the massive Literacy Crusade was launched. Actually, I didn't really understand what the revolution was all about, I suppose because of my father's attitudes and my conservative education, but I volunteered to go along to my father's village to teach the peasants how to read and write. I wasn't too good a teacher, but I began to realise how important it was for the peasants to read and write. It suddenly clicked – the connection between illiteracy and the terrible exploitation the peasants suffered under Somoza.

When I moved to Somoto to live with Mum I did some building jobs and got involved in the local Neighbourhood Committee to help do night-guard duty. I also helped set up our Sandinista Youth group and organise them to help on the coffee harvest because of the labour shortage caused by the war; and as my responsibilities grew I was awarded 'Militant of the Sandinista Youth'. Then I went to fight for four months in Jalapa. My first battle was near to San Ramon village where my brother had already been wounded in combat. I was dead frightened when we fought back these Contra; we tracked them down through the night. But the next day we walked right into their ambush! We fought for three hours until they retreated. We'd killed six of them. That was my first battle. When the bullets started I forgot I was dead thirsty and starving hungry, I forgot everything. My only thought was to stay alive.

I returned to civilian life after four months to pick up my old work with the Sandinista Youth and Neighbourhood Committee and worked in a bookshop selling revolutionary literature. But the people don't read much so we sold little. Then after a year I took up the offer to co-ordinate the youth study circles and production brigades. I joined the Sandinista Party in 1984 which led to my current political work in this battalion of the Patriotic Military Service near to Somoto. I have to maintain high political morale amongst the men and tackle problems like desertion, indiscipline and general bad behaviour. When we're not on the march I organise daily talks on what's going on in Nicaragua and give a class on politics twice a week; those men who prove themselves in good conduct and in learning receive some commendation. And when we're in action I have to guarantee the troops footwear, uniforms and ammunition and that payment comes on time. But it's when we're at base that I have to make sure the men don't get bored or homesick, so we've films and cultural events. But it's too much. I've let this work slip. There just isn't time to plan, and to be honest I often feel exhausted, my head completely empty, and then at other times I've got some brilliant ideas, but there they remain, just as ideas . . .

We've suffered a lot of damage in this region, and the Contra have grown into big task forces of 100 men or so, with their own regional commands. That's why we have to have the military service. Their aim is to exhaust us. They've tried taking towns here and want to set up a provisional government: that way they hope to get international recognition. Mum understands why I joined up; she's very busy too, what with the Neighbourhood Committee, her hospital union and the women's organisation. But you won't find many mothers wanting to see their sons in uniform, or women in the army. They aren't called up, they volunteer, and because many have to look after the children, they still see their place as in the home. Maybe they're still just underestimated; those women who are fighting are just as tough as the men.

THE DRY LEAF

José María Briones

A son of José María Briones, the late landowner of El Regadío, a farming community in northern Nicaragua.

My father, José María Briones, arrived in El Regadío about forty years ago. There were only four small houses then. People started settling here when he began growing sugar cane on a small tract of land and constructed the road from Sirena to El Regadío. Next he built one from El Regadío to Estelí. He had problems getting permission from other landowners to cross their land, even though he used his own money and tractor. He ended up buying it. Then he began rearing cattle. After twenty years the community had grown so much that he opened a school in his own home. As time went by there were so many children that, along with three other

An old man and pigs in El Regadío

Overlooking El Regadío

landowners, he financed the building of a new school.

He installed piped water in nearly all the homes – something which improved his farming as well. The chapel was built on land he donated and he built another road with government help, from the village to San Juán de Limay. Then, when the local people started making problems, he stopped giving milk to the mothers. They demanded a lot, I suppose because of this history of paternalistic relations.

The workers had small plots. It was a communal system of share-cropping whereby Father supplied seeds, oxen, manure and machetes and in return the workers gave him half their harvest. This wasn't considered fair after the revolution, so we changed, even though some still prefer the old way.

When Father died we sons inherited the farm, and in

Briones' cattle farm

about 1975 gave some land to the community, which they've developed with help from abroad. I also provided land for a health clinic to be built after the revolution. The clinic used to be in our farmhouse. We had a nurse who would call me in Estelí if she had problems since I'm a practitioner. I used to visit the village once or twice a week, until the people didn't need me any more because a Cuban doctor came, though I doubt he turns up regularly.

In my father's time we always helped out the workers with medicines and clothes, as well as paying some a wage. But times have changed and probably for the better. After the triumph some talked badly of my father. One farmhand said to me, 'If your father was alive today, he'd have us all hanged. He wanted all the land for himself.' Well, in the end he did own a great deal of land throughout the region. I suppose it's natural for people to criticise those who once held important positions.

In the end I gave some of the best irrigated land to the co-operative. I feel I have less right to the property nowadays. With these new ideals in Nicaragua my views have changed and I suppose the process will continue. To tell the truth, our relationship with Father was typically authoritarian. He hit us a lot and made us work: at fourteen I was ploughing with a tractor. I'd start at eight in the morning and work till six.

Some say I've sold out to the Sandinistas, others say I'm counter-revolutionary. Well, I'm working part-time and free of charge here in the Estelí hospital. I'm the only specialist. Few doctors have stayed behind. I was counting at mass yesterday and it's dreadful; out of thirty-five doctors there's only three left. As I studied in Spain I could easily work elsewhere, but I want to stay. Since the triumph I've earned very little, though I've sufficient for my two daughters to study abroad. They'll make up their own minds whether to return or stay away.

Adela Cruz

A peasant woman and mother of Otilia (q.v.) and eleven other children. She lives in El Regadío.

My mother taught me how to bake, help her make pots and bowls and collect the firewood for the kiln. I was twelve when I went to work for the Alegría family. I used to clean the floors, grind the maize and coffee, and cook

Otilia's mother, Adela, grinds maize to make the tortillas, with one of her daughters and child in the background

supper. And I had to work even when I was sick. Once when I refused, they took me off to the National Guard for a lesson.

I slept in their cheese dairy and drops of butter would fall on me. The place stank; it gave me bad headaches. With all the grinding I did I can still feel the pains in my hands.

Then I worked for Briones, cooking for fifty hired hands. It ruined my back. Briones wouldn't give me anything so I used to steal tortillas in my apron pocket and take the left-over junket for my children. If I got any credit in his store, I'd pay it back by doing extra work.

My husband worked share-cropping for Briones, which meant he got back half my husband's harvest. Later he threw my husband off the land when he brought in the cattle. It was then that my husband started drinking, morning, noon and night. In the end he left for Jalapa. He wanted to work for himself. Even today he's not interested in the co-operative. I kept going by making and selling bread – Otilia helped me. Then old Briones tried to evict

The local baker makes maize cakes

us, but I put up a good fight. He ordered the roof to be pulled down. Well, I just went and put a sheet up to cover us. He was a dreadful man. One evening, when Somoza came to visit Briones' farm, he came to get me to cook their dinner. My girl was sick so I told him I'd only go if he brought someone to mind the child. Well, he simply said that it was my problem and I had to come. Oh, I feel so angry for all that's happened! It's given me a bad temper.

When I had a miscarriage we asked Briones for his truck to take me to Estelí, and he refused. He took in everyone's harvests of maize, yet he'd have you begging hungry for days before giving back what was yours; and he had the nerve to say we ate like pigs. I remember the cloth I bought from him; it was so rotten that it just fell apart after the first wash. No cloth and no money! He didn't want us to be free, he wanted us to beg. It's not like that now. Now the maize belongs to me and I don't ask the rich for anything.

I spend my time looking after Otilia's little ones while she's out working. I wake at three and get to bed by eleven. I had eighteen children but was left with twelve, seven boys and five girls. Today some live in Estelí and some here, either working or studying. The first was born when I was fifteen years old.

When I was having my first child, José Leoncio, I went to stay at my brother's place. He was a farm manager and married with a child. Once, when he was off on some business, something really frightening happened. It was night, and we'd started a fire in the range, leaving the door open to let out the smoke. Suddenly, the dogs began howling and the children started to cry. There was a noise as if someone had fallen into the pond. I prayed to God, and told the children not to cry. And there, through the door, we saw someone on horseback. We prayed it was my brother, but it wasn't. It was the two hired hands of Briones who had drowned in the pond many years ago. Briones brought evil. Once in Briones' house I saw a strange woman dancing on the patio. They say the rich are close to the devil. Well, the devil took Briones in the end.

Spring 1984
Otilia Casco Cruz

A teacher and health worker and mother of five daughters.

This village was named El Regadío (Irrigated Lands) because with two rivers passing through it was always muddy and quite cool here. My father worked planting sugar cane, beans, rice, potatoes, plantains and cassava root. He was a share-cropper for José María Briones, the landowner, who was very rich and became a senator under Somoza.

We chopped firewood to sell. My mother used to wake at dawn to do the baking before going to help Father. It was different when I married – my husband paid a labourer because he didn't like me working in the sun – but when I was a girl it was hard. When Father fell ill we sold the sugar blocks cheap to Briones in order to have some money. People died because they'd no idea how to cure themselves and there were no medicines and health care available. They couldn't read so they even voted for Somoza. A lot of rum was drunk, especially during the San Antonio and Santa Ana festivals. But the men always ended up fighting, so the festivals were stopped. The women drank very little.

We lived in a house made of cardboard. It stank and our clothes were always dirty. It helped a little when my brothers started working, but then Father was thrown off the land and in the end left for Jalapa. We worked like oxen for the landlords.

My brother Miguel was killed when I was fourteen – my mother's bad luck. Miguel was walking through Estelí when a man asked him for a cigarette. When he went over,

Otilia hangs up the washing

the man stabbed him in the stomach. We got news he was in hospital the next morning and went straight there. He'd been killed by mistake because he had similar features to his cousin Sebastian, a lorry driver who had killed a girl crossing a road. Her father, a doctor who now lives in the United States, paid for Sebastian to be murdered. If you had money you could simply pay the National Guard to do your dirty work and all was kept quiet afterwards. There was no justice. In fact they nearly had my mother in prison: she went to the Estelí court over Miguel's murder and when she spoke up the judge told her to be quiet or she'd be sent down. José María Briones wouldn't even pay for my brother's coffin.

I did have happy times at school. We had a great teacher, Jaime Morales. He used to stand up for me when I got into trouble, and showed us a lot. He opened our eyes to the injustices we peasants suffered. He also gave us physical training every morning. My mates, Zacarias and Denis, reckoned he was giving us military training – and all under the nose of the National Guard – but they never guessed what was going on. Jaime also gave us books to read, like *The Hell of the Poor* by Reynaldo Antonio Tefel, who is now

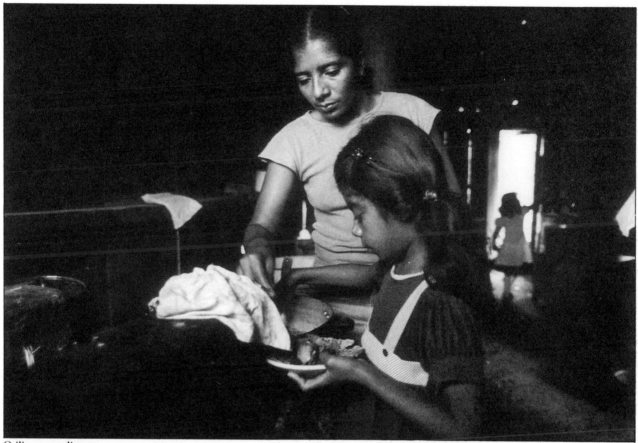
Otilia serves dinner

Minister of Social Welfare. Jaime disappeared after the police arrested him on a protest funeral march for José Ramón Barriente, who had been murdered by the Guard. They say Jaime went into exile in Venezuela, but who knows? My friend Zacarias Olivas became a great Sandinista fighter, commanding a division of guerrillas. He was killed in combat on 14 April 1979 in Rosario, in the Estelí region. And Denis Jarquín was also killed by the Guard.

After I left school I married Tacho. I was seventeen. His family helped us but the town's people didn't approve of the marriage because I was dark and came from a poorer family. We lived six months with my mother-in-law because we had practically nothing. Then Tacho's uncle Elicio Cruz asked us to move to his farm.

There Tacho met Martín Loza. This man had joined the Sandinista Front years back. He told us a lot about what they were fighting for in the mountains. He'd been a shoemaker in Estelí when he started collaborating, making boots for the fighters. He made a pair for Tacho when he started with the Front. We knew this struggle was for the people and that some day Nicaragua would be free. We

Otilia's daughter, Evelyn, sweeps the backyard

also learnt more when we went on a short course in Estelí where we related the Gospel to everyday life. After Martín, other guerrillas arrived. We'd feed them and off they'd go, up to the mountains. Many of these men are high-ranking officials today.

Up until then I didn't believe a revolution was possible. Ever since I was a girl I'd heard that the people would rise up against Somoza, but I only became certain of it when I actually saw the Guard massacre the peasants. Oh, terrible things happened before the triumph. A soldier raped a girl here; he cut off her breasts and drank her blood. It's because of all that I've gone through that I'm so clear today, and why I'm also a writer. I may have left school with little education, but I know a great deal. I may lack a lot, but each day is a lesson and a challenge.

We moved to another of Elicio's smallholdings which Tacho then managed. We reared cows, and had hens and pigs. We went on helping the Sandinistas and Tacho's uncle said nothing. After the land was sold in 1975 we worked as cattle-traders and rented a piece of land. When we had some money we bought our small house. It was just one room then, but we've since built on the kitchen and living room.

By September 1978 there were nineteen of us altogether collaborating for the Front in El Regadío. I handled the money to buy meat, beans and salt. I'd go to Estelí with my Marianela, who was three months old, and buy medicines to hide outside the village. When the final insurrection happened Tacho collected them to divide amongst the guerrillas and the community. We didn't have a doctor then, so only those able to read could tell what the medicines were good for.

About thirty men had gone to fight with the Sandinistas, including two of my brothers. The Sandinistas would turn up soaked through, and I'd start a fire in the back yard. They even brought in their horses. We used to chat and laugh about the Guard. There were six informers in the community, but we knew very well who they were. One was sent by the Guard to infiltrate the Front. He was dangerous, but nobody touched him after the triumph, at least not at first. Tacho said he should be let free. He was a distant relative of the family, but it was useless trying to

Otilia's children tidy up the bedroom

change him. He ended up in prison for throwing a bomb at the house of a Sandinista member.

After the triumph Juán and Tacho harvested their maize and beans to give to the people. Tacho went on farming and trading until he was called up and sent to the border to fight the counter-revolutionaries. I had the three girls and was pregnant again, so we had to live on savings. When he came back he helped organise the people to form a farming co-operative. Then after he was called up again he went to study for a month in Managua. It's because of the revolution that Tacho has been able to finish his primary education.

Soon after the triumph some of us women began work in the health campaigns. We went up to the village of Andes de Sandino. Everyone there was illiterate until the adult education classes began. The people said we were injecting their children with communism, can you imagine? We had to work so hard with these ideas of theirs. At times we just wanted to cry to see how scared they were, how they believed in God. They asked why we women carried guns and wore uniforms. We explained that there was danger in the area and we felt their children had the same

Tacho with Mari Carmen in his arms; below is Marianela. Lesbia is between Tacho and Otilia, who has Mercedes on her lap and with Evelyn to her right.

Otilia teaches Pancho, Tacho's father, and neighbours to read and write

right as ours to be vaccinated, especially as polio causes so much suffering.

The last time we went there was to promote the Patriotic Military Service, and some joined up. But many of these peasants joined the Contra in 1983. Now many have returned under the amnesty law. The people there are really confused. It's hard work, but I enjoy talking to them, trying to make them understand that the revolution is for them.

It's hard for many women to leave their children, especially peasant women, as they have so many. But we are thirty in the women's organisation, helping with health and education work. We're all friends and have a good laugh, joking about how, when our men come home from fighting, it's just another battle in bed. Oh, and we play tricks; we send anonymous love letters. But sometimes this can lead to an affair and I don't like that. I wouldn't do it, even though Tacho isn't here sometimes.

As a girl I was very naive about men. I was thirteen when our teacher showed us a book about what a woman is, and about menstruation and love at first sight. We made sure our mothers never found out. But when I married I soon realised I knew nothing about men or sex. People had told me sex was something powdery, so I thought it was like a talc, something one spread over oneself! Well, when the truth dawned, God help me, it was sad. I had no idea. You see, my youth was short-lived because of my brother's murder – we mourned for one year. My mother wouldn't

The primary school in El Regadío

allow me to go out with my boyfriend, or go to parties. I wasn't even allowed to ride horses. The women said there was no telling what might happen to girls on horseback. Some old belief that we wouldn't be the same. I only started to ride when I was married. All this was only said by those who couldn't read or write. You learn the facts with education.

Well, I remember when I married Tacho we went to the waterfall in the mountains, but I didn't want to bathe in front of him. I felt so ashamed. He told me I shouldn't feel this way, especially as we were quite alone with the birds, and that I'd have to change my ways, like flowers when they're pollinated. At night I only wanted him to see me with my clothes on, so he made me undress. He made me cry. Then he explained that marriage wasn't just passing time . . . That's for sure! We've been together for fourteen years now.

I'm sure Tacho didn't want to have children with other women, but before we married he did have another woman and they say she has a child by him. Before the revolution this child wouldn't have had any rights, but now fathers have to contribute financially to their children's upkeep.

I now think my children should have sexual education. I've read the women's magazine, Somos (We Are), which explains a lot. I teach the girls not to touch their private parts and they buy sanitary towels so they know about menstruation; even at their age they know about this hygienic method, instead of using rags. Contraception is available in the health centre and you can get the IUD in Estelí. I don't know what women took before to stop having children – maybe they used the pill or maybe only herbs.

Even these revolutionary men take advantage of women. It's better to stay friends and keep their respect. But there are plenty of women who have two or three men. To me they have no self-respect. I wouldn't trust them.

I can't say my friendships now are like the one I had with Zacarias. When we were children we used to talk about the guerrillas, about life. If only I'd been older I'd have gone to the mountains with him. Ah, all this; all those who have died have left their mark. I feel very deeply for this revolution. I can see my children will have a better life than us, because with better education they won't spend it all grinding maize, washing and ironing. The eldest, Leslie, is very clever. I hope she'll go to university, while the next, Evelyn, is rather slow and likes playing. Marianela is very naughty, but she says she wants to be a nurse like Susanna, a Chilean nurse who worked here, so she can care for me, she says, when I'm ill. Mari Carmen is only three – she likes singing and dancing – and the smallest, Mercedes, is only two so I cannot say. But I want them all to have a good education and I always try to give them guidance. Otherwise they might end up hemmed in at home.

Tacho wants me to study, too. Our friends are surprised, saying, 'How can you go off and abandon your children?' But I tell them that if the children are all right with me then they'll be all right with Tacho. We'll see how things turn out. I want to study next year, which should help me to write a book of poems on the story of our community. I've already written some showing how we raised ourselves out of such repression.

I'd also like to work in the co-operative, but there's too much housework to do. Out there it makes me feel good with the sweat on my brow. When Tacho married me he said he'd change my life. He made a great effort to make me happy, but he doesn't understand that my happiness is in writing and working the land. It's not that he holds me down, but I want to feel freer, to learn more. In fun he says I'd prefer a man's life, and then I tell him, 'No, it's that I've woken up at last.' I have to be honest that I don't feel really fulfilled working in the pre-school and adult education classes, plus the health work. It's too much of too little, although I know the work's important.

What's important, too, is that the co-operative grows; that more people join, and we produce enough for everyone . . . Tacho and I are here to stay, even if we get offered jobs in town.

The woman labourer

See the women workers
in the co-operative,
from sun to sun they toil
defiant of the bullets
to share out with love
the produce of their labour.

I so long, since we met,
to join you in the co-operative.
My love you have stolen
for all that has past
for your sacrifice and struggle
to destroy the powerful and mighty.

To them defence is crucial
as is the health campaign
these women are the fumigators,
and sowers of tobacco,
and if the ground is still not ready,
they then will drive the tractors.

These co-operatives are truly Sandinista
for they are the trenches of our education
defended surely by these women.
It is here they follow
from day to day
the path of Sandino.

After 50 years . . . Sandino lives on.

Otilia Casco Cruz

Tacho Olivas Cruz

The husband of Otilia Casco Cruz (q.v.). President of El Regadío co-operative and political worker.

During the first year after the triumph nothing was grown so we had to help each other with what we had. We all gave, even though we could have made a fortune from selling our maize . . . But what kind of revolution would that have been? I'm now thirty-two and feel so proud of what we've been able to achieve in Nicaragua. I've managed to complete my basic education and now we've got this co-operative. The government's helped us with finance and training and we also get technical advice. This has happened all over the country. These co-operatives are on lands that were under-used or abandoned. Before '79, when the peasants took over lands, the National Guard simply moved in to evict them. But not now.

Soon after the triumph, ninety men from Briones' farm

The co-operative

invaded his lands and took about 150 acres. Then the Sandinistas came to an agreement with Briones' son, leaving him with some land while the rest was legally handed over to the co-operative. There were fifteen of us, reservists, militias, members of the Neighbourhood Committee and the FSLN, and adult-education teachers, so with all those skills we easily organised the co-op, though two had to leave after six months to go and fight.

The work is hard and some of us aren't in good health, but it's going okay. This year we slaughtered 250 heifers and now the potatoes and maize are ready.

You'll find most of the people in El Regadío are with the revolution. There's always going to be people who don't agree with the changes, but we don't isolate anyone. Like, for instance, when the amnesty was given we said that anyone who had joined the Contras could return and be given the same treatment as the rest of us. Out of twenty men who joined the Contra, in one village near here, seventeen came back. That's some achievement. And we make sure to treat their families well.

El Regadío's Sandinista Youth giving a performance to celebrate national day in the new community hall

Winter 1984
Otilia Casco Cruz

A woman from one of the church organisations came to see us. We talked a lot and I told her how keen I was to improve health conditions here. So she asked if I'd go on a course about herbal medicines in Managua. The night before I was due to leave I couldn't sleep for worrying about leaving the children, but in the morning I decided to go and the children stayed with Mother. Well, it was really worth it; I learned such a lot and came out top of the class.

So then the organisation arranged for me to go on a second, more advanced course – in Mexico! I felt very bad leaving the girls a second time because Tacho had been mobilised and again I had to ask Mother to take care of them. It was a real job to get my passport in Managua, too, because I haven't got a birth certificate and all the offices were closed since it was the '84 elections. So the trip to Mexico was delayed. But once I got there I learned a good deal about acupuncture, massage and herbal medicine. It's so good that us peasants now have this chance to learn. But I remember I felt terrible as the plane took off from Managua. I wanted to cry thinking about the children when our village is so vulnerable to Contra attack.

Mexico City is just full of huge buildings and cars. It's very corrupt and the people go hungry. It's supposedly a revolutionary government, but there's nothing revolutionary about all that poverty. With all our suffering in Nicaragua no one goes hungry, nor are there the terrible illnesses you see in Mexico. The Indians are the worst hit, the Nahault and Tarahuamara people. On the course I met six Tarahuamara. They know a lot about medicines. They sell them in the United States as they live near the border, but they earn very little. They'll go hungry this year because it has hardly rained and the maize has died. They

Otilia collecting plants for her medicine

make clothes to scrape by, selling them cheaply to people who merely sell them again for a higher profit. They are very good and simple people, but oppressed. They hardly talked, not even with me. At the beginning of the course they ignored me – perhaps they thought I was like those Mexican 'revolutionaries' – but once I started explaining about Nicaragua they began talking. They're tough because of what they've gone through under the whites.

On the course I spoke about how we'd organised clandestinely. I explained about our President, Daniel Ortega, and how he'd fought for people's freedom; and about our campaigns for better health and education. I felt sad that some of these people were cynical. It made me think of the great silence on the buses in Mexico when no one talks to each other. You have to get around by reading signposts. When I was asked where I came from, at first I'd

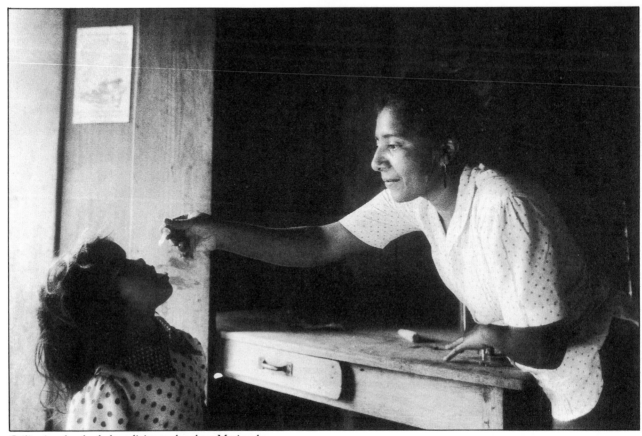
Otilia gives her herbal medicine to daughter Marianela

say Guatemala. Then I realised that was dangerous, so I said I was from Nicaragua, visiting my sister and seeing if I could stay in Mexico. If I'd said I was studying herbal medicines I'm sure they'd have thought I was a witch. We met a doctor called Eugenio Martínez, a very wise old man. He has problems in Mexico because his work in natural medicines threatens the big medical businesses. Such problems simply cannot happen in Nicaragua.

There's a secret struggle happening in Mexico. I met some very brave people and in some ways they suffer more than us with killings and kidnappings. One woman told me

about how her son was killed. She said it was part of the same struggle, that he'd died for the same cause. As I left she gave me a warm embrace and I thought of our mothers of the Heroes and Martyrs organisation. But their cause has yet to reach the people. During the Mexican revolution they awoke only to have their cause betrayed. I told them that in Nicaragua this was impossible – that we revolutionaries are part of the people.

I was also invited to speak to a group of representatives of the Contadora Group. I could hardly speak, but I did ask them, as 'concerned' people (I didn't say 'revolutionaries', because I knew I was dealing with officials), for their humanitarian support to end the war, so we could reach those people isolated in the mountains who needed medical care. They made me feel uncomfortable having to be so careful with my words.

I brought back a lot of books on herbal medicine for our library. Everyone was so pleased to have me home. The children were fine as Tacho had visited them on his leave from defending communities near to Estelí during this latest Contra offensive. I hope when the girls grow up they'll understand that we've done all this to make their lives better.

Summer 1985
Tacho Olivas Cruz

We now have enough cattle in the co-operative to supply meat and milk to nearly everyone in Èl Regadío, and it helps the other men when they need oxen to plough their lands. But I left the co-operative because there's now more important work to be done in the other communities nearby. It's delicate work: they haven't

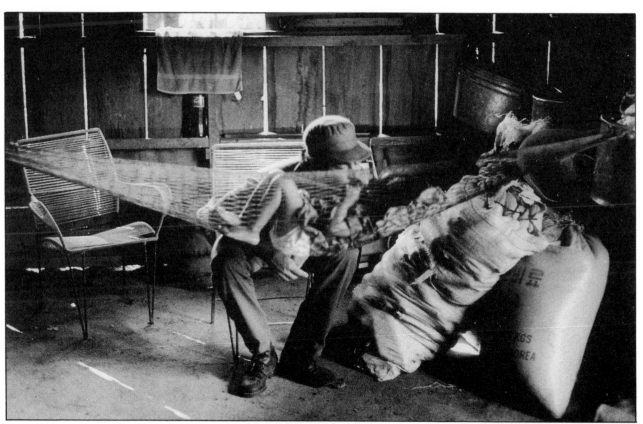

Tacho plays with Mercedes in a hammock captured from the Contra

received much attention until now, so many people aren't involved, and it's been easier for the enemy to work from the inside. It's when the people aren't organised that the Contra come in, capture men and take them into Honduras.

When I was last mobilised we men did a lot of talking on the march. Good men, but some had real troubles. One told me about how they'd received land from the Agrarian Reform but as none of them knew the first thing about running a co-op some got fed up and left, while the four who stayed on ended up in a shoot-out with local cattle farmers after they'd stampeded their cattle over the men's

The co-operative supplies meat to the community

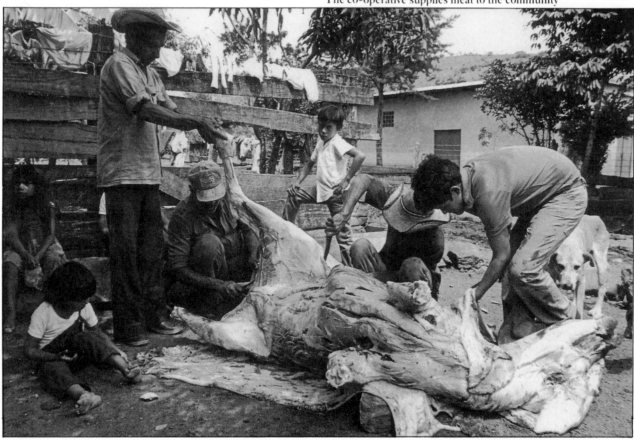

Tacho off to the communities

crops. So this is part of my work, to go up there and talk, and they all seem glad to meet. After all, they have to live together, and if we can't solve this amongst ourselves then I can take the matter to higher levels. But it's only by living here that you get to hear this kind of problem and can come up with real solutions. You see, this revolution wasn't made for one group to do well at the expense of others. That's what we're trying to do away with. Take our co-operative: it exists for all the families in El Regadío, it's part of the process, but it depends totally on our own effort. Take Ramón Rodrigues Casco. He came from a poor family near here – very good people. This was back in

Somoza's time. Ramón managed to pass his sixth grade and went to Estelí where he worked hard to continue his studies, but he ended up working in the Chinandega military base of Somoza. So after the triumph he was captured and held in Estelí. His family pleaded for the village people to petition for his release, so after forty-five days he returned free to his people. For one whole year we hardly set eyes on him, but then he took up teaching in the adult education classes, but he still felt nervous about visiting Estelí. Then we asked him to join the co-op, and he became one of the hardest workers we've ever had. But some members just wouldn't trust him with a gun or leave him to do night-guard duty. That changed the day he was kidnapped by the Contra and escaped back all beaten-up. Then he was given a gun and uniform, and now he's really one of us.

But this new work of mine has upset Otilia's plans to do regional health training, as she doesn't want to burden her mother with the children. So she's opted to make herbal medicines in the village. It's not even a matter of sharing out the housework, as I'm away for days on end; and even if I could do it, it's not that easy to clean the house after a hard day with the machete when we're worn out. We prefer to leave the dirt on our hands. I don't think a

Cleaning the rice

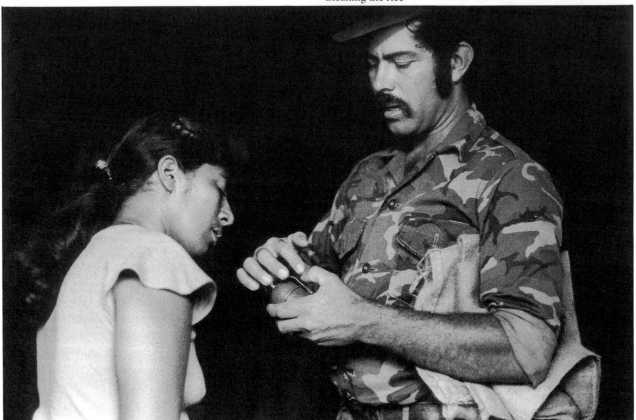

Tacho shows Otilia a grenade

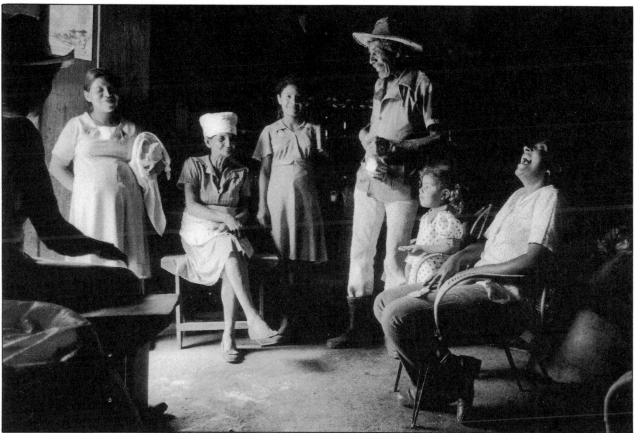

Otilia shares a joke with the newly arrived people displaced by the military offensive in 1985

woman's place is in the home, but there's plenty of Sandinistas who do. What's needed are more children's centres which would free Otilia. It's a real problem. Take this mother we want to help in the co-operative: she needs some training to do the job, but she's got a baby she can't leave so she won't get the job. What with parents who stop their girls getting on, frightened they can't take care of themselves, tell me, how are we going to have more women leaders? All the same, you can see these old macho ideas changing: so many women went to teach on the Literacy Crusade and go coffee picking every year.

Otilia Casco Cruz

The herb garden we've started here in El Regadío is the first in the region. Right now we can't make the herbal remedies for lack of alcohol and drop-bottles, but I manage to make medicinal tea by drying the leaves. So I feel all those dollars spent on my trip to Mexico have been worth it, because I've discovered plants here that can cure many illnesses. We've also begun collecting in information

Otilia's youngest brother (right) and another militia prepare their weapons for night-guard duty

from other women in the area to produce a book on traditional herbal medicines. Later on these women will teach other health workers. The Estelí hospital is going to use some of these remedies as a way of helping overcome the shortages caused by the US blockade.

At home we've been helping people displaced by the war with food and shelter. They're safer here. Our militias are good and we're quick to mobilise, but if the Contra ever caught us unawares and entered the village, they'd turn us into pulp.

There's still so much to improve in El Regadío. Often the village phone doesn't work and the roads here are in a terrible state. If the government didn't have to spend half the country's wealth on defence, by now all the homes would have drinking water and electricity. This war affects us all. I was going to teach other health workers how to use herbal medicines, but now Tacho is away that's become impossible. It would mean leaving the kids with Mother, which wouldn't be fair.

All this has made me think how much easier it was for

Tacho to become involved . . . he's had more opportunities to study since the triumph. It's the men, rarely the women, who are asked to attend courses. We're still stuck as housewives. I've told Tacho we women have been held back through all of history, and in these few years since the triumph not enough has been done to pull women up. Ah, there's plenty of blah, blah, about women's participation, but if a woman makes it, it's because she made sure not to bog herself down with a man and children.

We women are like dry leaves, while men hold on to their freedom. Take my sister: she used to be really involved in health work, but now that she's married her husband completely dominates her. He won't even let her out of the house without permission. And this abuse makes a woman underestimate herself. That man might be some big shot in the army but he's no saint when it comes to his family duties. Men have children with as many women as they can fool; well, that's why the laws are changing to try

Otilia and her friends washing in the pool

Outside José María Briones' farm

and stop all this irresponsible behaviour. But what's happened? Poor Mother ends up looking after all my sister's children, four of them. She could go mad. It's not right. It's her time to rest. A family should have more consideration towards its elders.

What a waste. Without love our spirit dies, like a leaf that falls into water and perishes to nothing. But then if it falls on to the good earth of love and care, it changes into rich soil, and of course there are couples who work well together in the revolution and in the home. But in general it's the men who have the freedom. They'll have to wake up and realise that women too should participate and live life to the full.

Otilia and her mother, Adela Cruz

The dry leaf

*Green leaves will perish
in the coming storm.
Your love betrays
as a broken dream
Caught in the winds
you fall with child
like a dry leaf
to barren ground.*

*Turn from false love
for you and your child,
to face the good sun,
and from repression
grow to replenish
our rich life around.*

Otilia Casco Cruz

Three-year-old Mari Carmen

THE FREEDOM TO CHANGE

María del Carmen López Calero

A mother of three, working at a printer's in the capital, Managua.

My proper name is María del Carmen López Calero, but friends just call me Carmen. My father worked the land and grew orange trees. My mother had twelve children because in those days women weren't told about family planning. After morning school we washed clothes and gardened and minded the animals. We were so poor there wasn't even enough to eat, so when I was thirteen I left home. In Somoza's time the capital was where the money was, so I came to Managua with a friend and found work as a housemaid, caring for two children and doing the washing and ironing. Then after three years I had the good luck to work for the secretary of the American Ambassador, following good recommendations from my previous employer. This meant I could help Mother as I earned a little more. They treated me well, gave me toothpaste, toilet paper and food. I liked that.

After the earthquake in 1972 they offered to take me to the United States, but I didn't accept. I was worried about my family and thought it might not be so easy to return to Nicaragua. But then I was left no better off, with no work and the little I had destroyed by the earthquake. I was forced to stay with my family until I found another job.

Some years later I started hearing about the Sandinista Front; that it was organising and fighting; and that the people were behind the struggle to get rid of Somoza. I had a close friend, Berta, who introduced me to people involved in the Front and employed me in one of their safe houses. At first I didn't fully grasp what was going on. Then one day one of the *compañeros* said, 'Carmen, do take care not to tell people what you're doing.' I asked what he meant, and he said, 'Well, you know, to be young today in Nicaragua is dangerous.' I wanted to find out more, so I talked to Berta. She said, 'Look, Carmen, how worthless our lives are. There have been too many martyrs. We can't give in to Somoza, we have to fight to get rid of him.' She went on, 'How many women never have an education? There are no grants, no promotion for workers, no freedom. We have a right to a better life and we're in the process of doing this, to liberate Nicaragua.' I liked what she was saying a lot, and felt really confident of these *compas*. I never told my man any of this, because I knew he'd be against my involvement – he was so macho. The *compas* took care of me when I got pregnant, and I kept on working. I badly wanted to study, but how could I when no college ran courses after eight o'clock at night?

The tension was building up. My brother had gone underground and Mother wasn't well. I visited her when I could, walking to the village with tradespeople. At home I'd say nothing about my assignment to my brother; that I was there to find out how the people in La Concepción were participating in the struggle. Neither did he tell me of his own involvement, maybe because he thought I might tell Mother. What a situation! I couldn't tell him what I was doing for security reasons and I remember him accusing me of getting used to the city bourgeois way of life. He said, 'Soon you won't even care for your own people.'

I used to return to Managua by horse and cart from La Concepción, passing the Santiago Volcano. I slept at Berta's. She had four children, including a baby, and we agreed that if ever she was killed I'd take care of the children and go on with the work.

Around that time something very sad happened. The father of a friend of mine was picked up by the Guard after they discovered arms on his farm. What had happened was that a collaborator had been caught leaving the farm with a sack of charcoal with two rifles inside. The Guard tortured him so badly he nearly died. This led to the old farmer's arrest, but he knew nothing about it all. When we took him food to the prison, the Guard there said to us: 'Your old man isn't going to get this food. He should die. You scruffs had better learn not to help these Sandino communists. The day the communists rule here you'll be the first to go because only the rich and ambitious will have power.' Well, in the end my friend's brother managed to obtain the

Carmen's mother and daughters prepare dinner to have in their garden in La Concepción

father's release. I don't know how. This was six months before the triumph.

There were other difficult times, for instance when our security house was broken into. One of the *compas* accused me of leaving the door open, unlocked. The television, clothes, iron, books and, most serious, important papers were stolen. They thought that perhaps I was an infiltrator. I was very shocked. They sent me away for five days as punishment. I thought they might even kill me, so I went to my father's in La Concepción where I'd be safe, but I told my family nothing.

Then after the five days I resolved to show the *compas* that I was reliable and committed and decided to return. In fact, while I was away they'd discovered that the Guard had broken in through the bathroom and they asked for my forgiveness for having accused me. They began to trust me much more and I was soon given full responsibility for money matters and food distribution to other safe houses. If we got hold of clothes we'd send them to the boys fighting. All the while I kept on washing and ironing.

We moved several times because of security problems. Once we discovered our landlady was the mother of some

Carmen's niece, nephew and son watching a militia man on television in Carmen's mother's home

big military character, so we moved fast to reorganise the arms cache and meeting centre. Finally, when the big strike happened in 1979, we felt we were close to winning, and produced propaganda calling on the workers to unite.

By June I was heavily pregnant again, so the *compañeros* sent me to a farm outside Managua for more safety. Even so, it was near a military training school. I kept on working as a messenger; sometimes I would meet collaborators on the same mission, but we wouldn't let on until past all the road blocks. Then I'd perhaps say, 'Look, take this gun, hide it for a week and then take it to the Sandinistas.' We were always crossing each other's paths.

Then came the triumph: a day of great happiness. There was such joy that Somoza had gone. I was outside Managua on the main southern road. People were clambering on to any passing transport to get down to the Plaza for the celebrations. Well, blow me if I didn't get on to a lorry driven by the National Guard! I thought something was up when they turned off the Managua road. They were using us as camouflage to make their get-away, but once they reached the quiet road they let us down. While we were waiting there I heard shots, and the next thing we saw the Sandinistas were driving them back, captured. They probably took them to the Chipote command post, and I hope they're still there.

Eventually we reached Managua for the great celebration. But there was still work to be done. The very next day I met up with the *compas* to find out who'd been killed during the insurrection. I was terribly upset to be told that one of my friends had died on the retreat of the Managua population to Masaya. Now grief has become a part of everyday life – to hear that this friend, that soldier, or workmate has been killed in some Contra incursion or ambush . . . But then you look on the bright side and see friends like Berta who has moved on and today works in the women's organisation.

The *compas* helped me by finding me work at a printer's. I started as a cleaner, but soon moved into the photo-mechanics section. When the workers there saw how quickly I learnt they suggested I join the production team in the collation section, taking on one of the machines. So far I've learned to run a folding machine and the saddle-stitcher. When I started the other women asked how I could do the job, as the machines look so complex and heavy. They were really surprised when I showed them I was capable of doing so-called men's work. In the past there was talk only of the 'workman', never a mention of the woman worker. The women's organisation has demanded that women be given better access to training and skilled work.

We have plans to build a library as a place to sit back and read and hold meetings. We'd also like a small clinic because a health check-up here revealed that lots of workers have blood problems, nervous conditions and headaches caused by chemicals and lead inks, and the heat is dreadful. We've asked for protective clothing as well.

As the union says, our strength is in our organisation, and we must keep a grip on this to maintain decent wages. We're not working for a boss like we were before. This is our own printworks to look after. We take turns to do night-guard duty to stop sabotage and robberies. We've had three robberies here, so we have to be careful.

Sometimes I think our Commander, Tomás Borge, was too generous in letting so many National Guard free and leaving really reactionary people to carry on working inside the country. It has certainly affected the printworks. There are people who've worked here for twenty-five years, and the Front has never tried to get rid of them because the revolution favours the working class and has never aimed to destroy its people. But then what do you do with these reactionary types? They constantly obstruct so many good plans. Take the Patriotic Military Service. My brother is mobilised, which we consider to be important as Nicaragua needs to be militarily strong for those gringos to see we're united and able to put up a good fight. But what do these old folk say? 'Why not send Tomás Borge and the rest of them up to the border to fight their enemy, that's their problem, not ours?' And when it's time for coffee-picking it's always the same young workers who volunteer. The others bicker: 'Since when did Somoza expect us to go coffee-picking free of charge?'

Well, I stick to my guns. I want to run other machines as well, and I'll earn more – which I need with prices rising.

My life is improving. After the triumph I lived with my husband in the countryside. I'd set off at four in the morning to catch the bus. I'd finish work at five in the afternoon and be back by eight. It was tough going, so I asked the Central Neighbourhood Committee in Managua if they could give me this plot in town where I'm living today. I made this home myself. There I was with the children, in the sun and rain with nothing but a bed, building this room around us. Then my husband came and joined me.

I felt better being closer to the works, but the children were left on their own, so for their sake I decided to do the night shift while my husband worked the day one. But I fell ill from only having four hours sleep and with all the washing and cooking to do as well. So after a year I sent the two girls to Mother and the boy stayed here, and I went back on to the day shift. At weekends I visit the girls with the boy. The rest of my spare time I spend doing voluntary work in my neighbourhood.

Now that I've just separated from my man it's much easier to go along to meetings. Before whenever there was

Carmen organising a sanitation clean-up of the printworks

There's always some conflict in the home. Sometimes the man is too macho and the woman has to fight and fight for some freedom. For all my efforts, my man only got worse, drinking every day, pouring our wages down his gut, and the children were upset. They'd say, 'Good, the old drunk is so gone he won't make it home tonight.' I felt nervous too. I'm still frightened he'll roll in drunk some night. In the end I told him to choose between me and the bottle, and he chose the booze. Perhaps I'm a little harder up, but at least I feel calmer and the children are more secure. I've moved on. We fought over politics, his vices, bad behaviour and character. I've said, 'We'll never

A couple move into their home in Carmen's neighbourhood

a woman's meeting my husband would try and stop me. Well, I used to tell him, 'I am going, because I'll certainly find better people there than I do here.' And off I'd go. The meetings took up a lot of time, but oh, they were worth it. Our women's organisation has achieved something with these new laws, like the one to promote equal relations between father, mother and child; and the other important one on parental responsibility for children, whether born in or out of wedlock. That's a breakthrough all right. Despite being separated, my man still has to contribute financially to the family.

Carmen working on the folding machine

understand each other, but let it be clear, I'm no little woman, and if you don't want to understand me it's because you don't love me.' He said, 'That's fine. It's your decision.' But now he's sorry. The mates at work have told me he misses the children.

We were together for twelve years – I was only eighteen when we met and had our first child. During the war the *compas* said there was no more room for machos and urged me to speak up against him. But he'll never change.

My concern is for the children's education. My boy has problems and I'm taking him to a psychiatrist. Next year when the eldest girl comes back to me she can care for the smaller ones and study in the evenings. I hope she can be independent and eventually get a grant to go to university. I'm gentle with the children, to let them come into their own. When I was young we were always getting a flogging.

My husband has been so negative and self-destructive. My workmates have told him that I've helped a lot at the works and I've got their support. 'We know you've tried to destroy her,' they've said. They know how he's held me back. Well, now I'm free to move on and he knows my mind is made up.

WOMEN WORKERS ORGANISE

Alicia Andino

A single mother in her early twenties who works in the tobacco factory in Jalapa near to the Honduran border. She is a union representative and local reporter for the Union of Agricultural Workers (ATC).

Here in Jalapa most of the men have been called up and the women have stayed to work on the farm. They do the militia duty there too. Every day we hear shots and mortar fire in the distance and we've lost some of our men. It's a sad situation. Many of these Contras are just ordinary poor people who've been kidnapped and forced to fight. They're not really our enemy.

The economic blockade affects us all, especially because in Nicaragua we can't make all the machines we need. But we won't starve – tobacco lands are being turned over to corn production, not only for what we need here but for the whole country.

Because of the war, peasants have moved into the town, and now we've got new settlements around Jalapa. The only people left along the border are those defending the country. In '85 lots more families had to move here because there was a major offensive against the Contra. When they first came they had to sleep in tents. They were really bitter about leaving their lands, but through a lot of hard work they've managed to build new homes. The men have started working in the farming co-ops. They have their own plots, too, so they've soon seen results. The most important thing now is to build the children's dining rooms and see how the nursery schools can cope with the new kids so that they start learning when they're young.

With time most have adapted and some have even joined the militias. That's a big change for people who've lived completely cut off, who hardly knew we'd had a revolution.

I suppose my involvement started well before 1979 when I met some people who told me about the Sandinistas. I was so naive. I remember asking one of these women if I should vote in the Somoza elections. Then I began to learn that the Sandinista struggle was for people like me: the working class.

There was no work here before the triumph so I had to go to Honduras and leave the children behind. It was tough. After the victory I returned and got involved in a mass of activities and planning. I was right in there. I wanted to know everything that was going on. Mother didn't like me being out at night, so I couldn't go to evening meetings. She had a weak heart and was nervous, so it was difficult. After her death I began working day and night. I was helping to set up a local theatre group with some really great people, making costumes and putting on benefits to pay for the house belonging to the women's organisation in Jalapa. I started work in the tobacco factory and stayed there for more than five years and taught in the adult education programme as well. I learnt as much from them as they did from me.

Then the union asked me to work as one of their local reporters and I began to appreciate much more the common problems that we tobacco women face – all the housework, children and husbands who stop us getting

Out of a population of three million, 250,000 people have been displaced by the war

Refugee children's party, and men clearing ground for their co-operative in El Portillo settlement

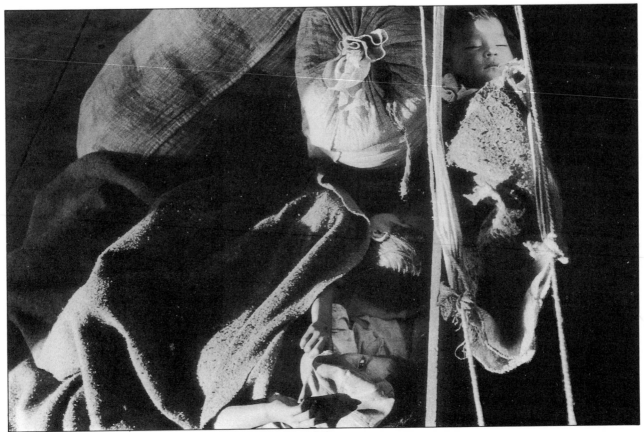

Children displaced by the war sleeping in La Estancia settlement, Jalapa

involved in outside activities. At meetings I've tried to encourage the women, saying how terrible I felt when I found myself pregnant with my third child. But then I decided not to let it change my life, or interfere with my other activities. I decided to get up earlier to prepare the kids' food and get all the cleaning done. And it's worked out fine.

The union work has been marvellous. It was certainly tough going at first, but we've set up a kitchen garden and we'll have the work canteen built soon. We made a big effort to build the children's centre; I can't count the number of times I went to meetings about this in Estelí. Now the children are well looked after and the centre stays open extra hours when there's overtime in the tobacco fields. Pregnant women, too, now have monthly check-ups and get three months' maternity leave, and if a mother takes time off because a child is ill she doesn't have her pay docked.

Some of the women tobacco sorters suffer eye infections from the nicotine fumes in the air, and some have lung problems because they don't like wearing cotton masks which make breathing harder. As a result, the union has

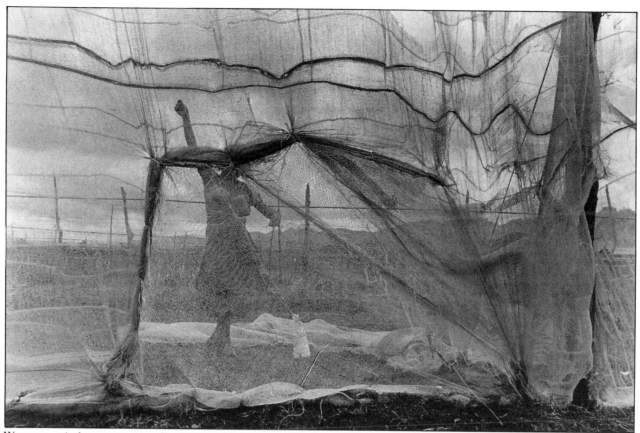

Women repair the gauze netting that protects the young tobacco plants. In the background are the Honduran mountains

arranged for workers to have regular medical check-ups and for an optician to come in, but really we need a better ventilation system.

At union meetings we discuss current events and women's issues. But many women are shy and don't ask questions or say what they want. That's why the union has started a project to deal just with the women workers. Every regional office and workplace will have its own woman rep. It'll be difficult to get in all the information on women's problems but what we want to do with union backing is to have the women workers organise themselves throughout Nicaragua so they resolve their own problems, whether these are about education, health, domestic conflicts or, say, child care.

Men union reps tend to ignore the women's problems, even though these may affect their work. You won't find out anything by sitting in an office and thinking everything is okay. Well, we've some very warm-hearted and outgoing women in the union and they're the ones who can best talk with the women workers and find out what's really going on. You know what I think we need? To sit these men down so that their women can tell them that we're not just born to be slaves and bring up the kids alone. It's the men who have to change. Even the revolutionary men. Not long ago the women here organised their militia battalion, but some left because they were frightened their men wouldn't look after their children. But never mind the militias – try going to a party alone and not getting a beating from your husband when you get home!

As for my men, they all bossed me. I left the father of my last child. What's the point of being with a block who grunts at you and yells for his dinner? Imagine your so-called 'loved one' telling you not to work if you don't get paid for it. My reply to him was, 'Well, if you won't bring in

Women set off for the fields at six in the morning

Women repairing the gauze

the maize you can't want any maize cakes, so that will save on my baking.' If I'd stayed, I'm sure I'd have withered away. Anyway, I feel so much better now I'm on my own. I'm learning so much. If I ever found another man he'd have to be a really good friend, a good laugh and understand about women's rights.

My children are really proud of me. I've even heard them say, 'She does so much, and she's on the radio because we've heard her.' I feel so happy they're growing up this way, learning not only in school but from their mother as well. That's important, to involve them in your outside life with your own friendships and concerns.

Women are so often hampered by six, seven or even ten children. They'll often hit their children for the slightest thing because the mother feels worthless. I used to hit my children too. I was stifling them, not allowing them to play and enjoy themselves in case they got dirty. Once I gave my eldest girl such a spanking when she skived off school. How was spanking going to help her learn? So then I spoke to her, saying, 'I want you to have an education, to be able to learn more than me and do more with your life.' And it worked; she feels loved and has pushed on in her class. Life always gets better if you set your mind to it.

For three years I've been saving up to have my own

A tobacco worker sews up the leaves before they are hung to dry

house built. Since Mother died I've been living with my sister, and have started to save by buying two piglets which I fattened up and sold. With the profit I bought some more and when they were good and fat, I sold all but one, which had six more piglets, so I sold them and so on. I've never touched a penny of the pig money, it was the Saint's Blood. I feel really happy because once you're independent in your own home no one can interfere with the enjoyment of your children.

Yes, it's good. I like my work too. Now I'm teaching other workers to become local reporters. Being local, people tell me their worries. Some of the important news

Alicia takes notes on the way people are settling in to their new community, El Portillo

Alicia and one of her sons

Tractor-drivers, with Victoria Torres in the centre, chatting after their mechanics class in Jalapa

gets national coverage. We have regular meetings where reporters from the union farms pool their information. It's a real encouragement for people to hear themselves over the radio, and especially for the women when they hear about things involving them. This never happened before. I've learnt something through this struggle – still not enough I should add – but I feel my eyes are opening. I'm learning that this revolution is what we make it . . . and the serious problems we face, they get harder every day.

I'm clearer and more decisive. Some changes came easy, some with blood, sweat and tears, but I've found freedom working for this revolution and no one can take that away. Once I never dared raise my hand and question what was going on. Now we question everything.

Victoria Torres

Victoria Torres is a tractor-driver on the tobacco-farming collective of La Mia in Jalapa.

Because of the draft the union asked if I'd like to drive a tractor. I made myself get behind that wheel and taught myself. Nowadays they teach women. Before, I used to do the fumigating and sew and bind tobacco.

There's an awful lot of work and we often stay on till

Victoria Torres waits for the Sandinista troops to pass by

well into the night. We've had our troubles; one of our women was killed when her brakes failed. Also the men were taken aback at first to see us women drive, but now they're fine and help a lot. We're doing a mechanics course, since we've ruined tractors in the past for lack of maintenance. I've picked up a few tips so I can fix the tractor myself. That's always been a man's secret. Ah, we women are getting on. When the men come back from the fighting we'll all work together.

I earn very little because I only do trailer work. Those who plough and sow earn more. Only new men earn as little as I do, and some even earn more, despite doing the same job. I have enough just to buy food. They don't even give us boots; to buy my clothes I eat less: I only eat beans. In two whole years our team manager hasn't given me any promotion – that's for the men only. We've complained about this to the union, who are talking to him. His excuse is that there aren't enough implements and that women don't like working. He says you need balls to work, but just look at me; I give it all I can. On other farms the women tractor-drivers are doing fine. It's just this fellow who has a problem with women.

Flor Ramírez

The head of the tobacco section of the Union of Agricultural Workers (ATC).

I was born and raised over El Crucero way, near Managua. We were eleven kids and, as the eldest, I had to help my parents with the housework and in the fields. I got a little schooling when I was twelve. All my spare time was spent in going to class, and by the time I was fifteen I could read and write. Then I fell in love with a cane-cutter and we married and went to work on the coffee plantations. It was a miserable existence. We didn't have our own home and had to live in workers' quarters. Women earned half a man's salary for doing exactly the same work. We'd work from five in the morning to five in the evening, then make the kids' supper and Lord knows what else while the men sat back waiting for their coffee to be served.

Both my husband and I were brought up in the Evangelical faith, but my ideas began changing when I met

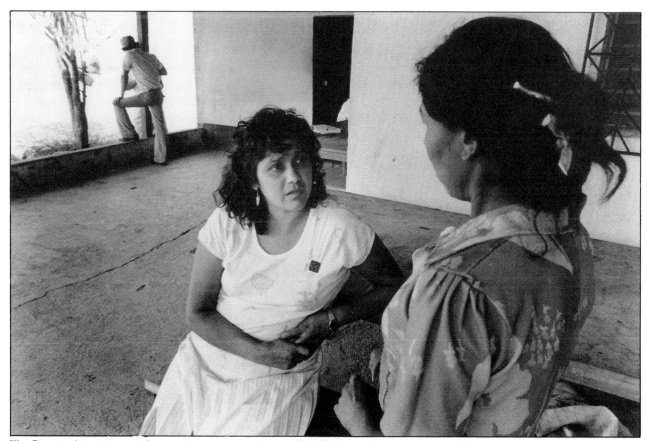

Flor Ramírez listening to a tobacco union representative near Estelí

some friends who were involved in the Sandinista revolutionary movement. By 1977 our first peasant movement got going and the Farm Workers' Committee was formed through the Front. My husband was very traditional and said we'd be better off staying out of trouble. The church made the Sandinistas out to be communist monsters, so I became involved secretly. The Front opened up a whole new world, helping me to understand more clearly how the system worked, how the landowners exploited us, and how Somoza waged war against anyone who opposed him, while he and his cronies dined off golden plates. What a life, picking coffee, lugging sacks, all for a few measly pennies, and always in debt to the farm stores – the Rats, as we called them. Any questioning and you'd end up with no job at all, blacked from all the farms, your only option being to turn to crime or prostitution, or else join the struggle. Not everyone in El Crucero joined the struggle, out of fear or not recognising their own suffering: but those who did are today fighting the Contras in the mountains. Many have become good leaders; although my husband didn't join them then, he's a lieutenant today.

After the triumph, I helped organise the union on the farm and promptly got the sack for my efforts. They gave me 10,000 *cordobas* redundancy pay to be rid of me. I'd never seen so much money. I'd never had a penny to my name before, only my kitchenware, a suitcase of clothes and my kids. It was like winning the bingo. I went straight to market, bought a bed, some chairs, pots and pans . . . I went crazy, and with my new home all set up I carried on working for the Union of Farm Workers. In those days everyone complained that policies were unclear. It was a big mess. I then moved to another coffee farm owned by a Turk to organise there, and was elected General Secretary of the union. The boss was underpaying so I called a strike. Five hundred workers came out, and we won our demands. I'd had my fill of these bosses and gave it all I could. Word started spreading to other farm workers and soon everyone

wanted me to come and set up their union for them. But the union invited me to head office and asked me to take on union organising in the whole Crucero area. We used to kick out any boss who refused to pay the stipulated wage. They'd panic, but we made them shape up or else hand over the farm.

Then, in 1973, the union sent me on an agricultural technical course to learn economics, politics, administration, accountancy and statistics. Despite my little education I passed with flying colours. Of course it was a hard slog and at times I felt very alone. That's when the problem started with my husband. He didn't like me going out, wearing trousers, using make-up, with my hair cut short, and mixing with other people. Though he eventually came round to understanding the revolution, he was still very macho. He had to be the one in charge. He couldn't accept me coming in late from meetings or going off on some union work for a week. It came to the point where he said, 'It's me or the union', so I told him it was the union. His jealousy and pride were killing him. We were getting on really badly and it was upsetting the kids. He knew I loved him but that I'd go where the revolution needed me, and in the end we separated.

I wouldn't say things are perfect now, looking after the house, helping the kids with their education, scraping enough together for clothes and food plus doing the job on top. I think women, especially Nicaraguan women, are very proud. I told my husband not to worry, I'd earn enough to take care of the children and I haven't asked him for a penny. Luckily I haven't fallen in love again.

Some women depend on their men, and put up with beatings. My husband and I used to fight, but he'd never struck me except once when he came in furious and hit me on the nose and it started to bleed. I was pregnant at the time. I grabbed a battery and clobbered him across the head with it. That cured him: he swore never to lay a finger on me again. But there are women who aren't in control of their lives. If their men don't want them sterilised they aren't, and if they want them to keep on having children they simply do. If I see a woman is being put down I speak up for her. We let our feelings be known and claim our rights in the union. But at a national level women workers have to define and prioritise their major problems. The union women's project has completed the first stage of a survey and research, and now we're on to the second stage of training women trade unionists in the regions to organise women workers to defend their rights.

In Nicaragua we're beginning to tackle the need for sex education. Just imagine, had I been taking the pill I would never have had seven children. Now I'm more in control of my life, but that's me. Many others aren't, and abortion isn't the answer. Both men and women need sex education. Some women tell you it's God's will. Is God going to provide dinner for all her children? I'm not criticising anyone's belief, let them believe in the devil, but we want to have the choice whether to be pregnant or not. I mean, if the conditions aren't right because of the war and economic blockade, why the hell burden yourself with another mouth to feed? Now we women are trying to get a law passed to make abortion legal. We don't want any more

The Jalapa ATC woman's project rep, Victoria Gomez, speaking at a local union meeting

back-street abortions. This happens when women are desperate, when your bastard man leaves you or refuses to take responsibility, and you can't carry on working and don't want to turn to crime. Then the only alternative is the back-street abortionist: the so-called midwife drops in, sticks a needle up you, and maybe pierces you instead of the foetus. All she's interested in is money, and what happens after? Vaginal infections, tumours, sometimes the women need an operation and have to be treated by the national health service, at its expense, costing ten times as much as having the abortion legally in a hospital. If you visit the women's hospital, Berta Calderon, you'll see loads of women there with fallen wombs, infections and all sorts of complaints. So we're hoping the law will come down on our side.

There are other laws that need changing. At present the Ministry of Housing gives priority to married couples with children, but there are plenty of single mothers and women who want to live together. Single women working for the union out in the regions are living out of suitcases. We hope the National Assembly will support us to change this.

Plenty of other people remain blindfolded by past values, like my mother. She told me that I always had to obey my husband, and always stay faithful, even if he died. I ask you! But question the man: no way. Men's attitudes were part of the vicious discrimination against women under the dictatorship. Women never used to have a say like they do now. I never spoke up: I went dumb. I got so nervous whenever I had to talk to people, and now I talk more than a parrot. I'm no intellectual and talk a bit plain, but I'm afraid of no one. At this year's Women's National Assembly I even told our Commander Bayardo Arce that I thought he was up the spout on women.

That would never have happened in Somoza's day. You'd never have seen some common upstart shouting her mouth off; the Guard would have beaten the living daylights out of me. Whereas at the Women's National Assembly we talked straight; 'Look Commander, what

we're proposing is this, and you . . .' Intellectuals and ordinary women alike all let ourselves be heard. We have a voice and a vote, and we're listened to. But you can't expect all the problems to be solved overnight. That'd be absurd. But step by step, for the first time in history, women are gradually filling positions of authority. Take our union, I'm head of the tobacco production section and there's a woman in charge of the women's project; the administrator is a woman, and Rosario is in charge of staff problems and promotion, and so on. That should give you an idea of where we're going.

We don't want matriarchal domination, but equality. Men's attitudes haven't changed drastically as yet, but there are exceptions like my son. He's in the military, but when he's on leave he does the mopping, sweeping, carries in the water, chops wood, starts the fire and does all sorts of work he'd never touched before. I mean, a man with a broom in his hand! In Somoza's day that was unheard of.

There's a long way to go on all fronts. It's not all roses, what with bosses taking advantage of the revolution and religious leaders using the church against the process, and you can't tackle them head-on. But we're clear where we're heading. If not, we'd have been crushed by now. And it's a clarity that comes from practice, through political and cultural education, and through fighting for our rights. Before the unions were ineffectual, but since 1979 they've gone from strength to strength. It's easier to implement our demands on the state farms, but with tough talking the union also gets wage regulations enforced on the private farms.

We're restructuring the union to represent the workers according to their agricultural sector, in coffee, tobacco, cattle and sugar; and we union reps are taking courses in production so as to learn the whole process, from the tobacco field to its sales, from the tobacco planter to the dock worker. We'll be better equipped to represent the workers' interests, and as they tell us what's happening on the ground nothing will slip our attention, whether it be

Youngsters working part-time on a tobacco farm

mismanagement, labour problems or shortages of spare parts.

The fight for decent wages and housing, and for health and educational services is a fight against the blockade and the war. These terrible long sheds where the coffee workers and families sleep won't disappear overnight, nor will child labour. But at least we can make sure the children earn the same as the adults, and work a half day so they get schooling. Because they help the family income, we often have to convince the mothers of how important it is that their children get an education.

The blockade affects all agricultural exports: cotton, tobacco and sugar. The Estelí cigar factory is working part time and some *compas* were laid off. The war has a bigger impact, with the precise intention of fucking us up. We've got to pull this thorn out. They're not going to crucify us, no way. We've got guts, and I assure you no one will starve here, even if we only have beans and rice to eat. When I was a child we lived through a dreadful crisis. Coffee prices plummeted and the people were crying with hunger; the workers and peasants were starving, yes madam, we were! So if we survived that in times of dictatorship, tell me

Victoria Torres on the tractor waiting for rice sacks to be loaded

why we can't survive now when we have a government that belongs to the people, who are giving all they can?

In the end things will get better in Nicaragua; we'll achieve socialism, but this needs economic growth and won't happen through some decree. We're criticised by the far left and right, by everyone, but we can't get there alone. We're underdeveloped, with no machinery, so it's bound to be a slow process. But we carry on, battered and bruised. Maybe it will take ten years, maybe twenty, before workers and peasants achieve their rights, but we'll keep right on.

Our union *will* end poverty – there will be no more barefoot workers or child labourers. But first the war must end, and everything depends on defence and production. One cannot exist without the other. Soldiers cannot fight if they are hungry, and the farms need protection from the Contras. In the end the US has two options: to exterminate all of us, or leave us in peace to carry on. But in the meantime we go on dancing and living life beneath the bullets. It may take another thousand or fifty thousand lives, but we'll get there. Our children *will* live a better life.

I don't know if I'm proud, but this revolution is like none other. We're a small nation, but we're courageous and sharp. We have to be, because other people, oppressed as we were once, see in us a way forward, like a mirror. Mistakes have been made, but they haven't been hidden and because our cause is just and honest we're an example to the Latin American people. They gain moral strength from us to fight for their own independence. We won our freedom, not with treaties, or flowers, but with suffering and bullets. Nothing was given, and so we tell our Latin American brothers and sisters that they too are strong and can fight. We give them our spiritual morale.

Bomb shelter beside the school on La Estancia settlement

The children's dining room in La Estancia settlement

SELF-DETERMINATION

María Borjas

A peasant woman from Ocotal and mother of Rosario Antunes (q.v.).

I was born on 31 March 1901. I'm every bit as old as the century. I didn't have any schooling. It's the wear and tear of life and the passing of the years that have given me a few notions.

I've always felt a lot for Sandino. My family was Liberal, so I grew up with that way of thinking. In those days in Ocotal there were few like us; people were mostly Conservatives. The Liberals eventually won their revolution when Moncada became president in 1929. It was around that time, in 1927, that Sandino appeared. He occupied the San Albino mine this side of El Jícaro and rose up in arms. By that time the old Somoza, father of Somoza Garcías, was already serving in the army.

Sandino passed by twice going from Jícaro, recruiting men. I used to see him because I lived off the turning from Ocotal in a place called El Deslizadoro. The people were always saying, 'Sandino is coming', but you never believed them until he finally did. He launched an attack from there on 16 July, and that morning I saw him from very nearby. Sandino's troops swarmed in on horseback. He killed a lot of marines; it was a massacre, but Sandino's men suffered more than the gringos. At dawn they were still fighting, and continued until three in the afternoon. Then Sandino withdrew. This was when I saw planes for the first time. They came in the morning and then later in the afternoon. And since then the planes have stayed.

But in the end the gringos defeated the poor fellow. He did a foolhardy thing: he went to make friends with the president, and that's how they murdered him. Somoza, the father of those crooks, was the one who killed him.

It was horrible when the Americans came to Nicaragua. It was then that prostitution sprang up. The gringos would kick the doors down and break in to rape us, so we had to arm ourselves with machetes and knives, whatever we could lay our hands on. That frightened them. But the gringos remained here, controlling the government. The government and the National Guard, along with the Somoza family, owned all the bars and the flesh of these poor prostitutes. When the gringos left, Somoza's men took over, licensing the bars and the women. It was a terrible time with drunken naked women getting up to all sorts in the streets. The Guard used to kill people, kill anyone at the drop of a hat. And it never made the news. They weren't punished because they were the Guard. Nobody talked about Sandino, nobody was allowed to, because they'd blow your head off if you did. You know, it was the Americans who cut up their victims.

The landowners took the peasants' lands and even their huts, everything. At that time my mother fled to Honduras, but I stayed behind in Ocotal. I was living alone, looking after my daughters. My father had died when I was sixteen. I worked for a rich family, grinding coffee, ironing and making maize drinks and tortillas. Clothes and hardware were brought up to Ocotal on mules from León every six months. We used to save our pennies to buy the closely woven cloth. Everything was transported, including sugar and rice.

I was forty-seven when I met my second husband. I had nine children, but three of them died. The last two, María and Rosario, were by my late husband. When we had María, he said we should marry. Then when we had Rosario we separated, but we ended up together again, working to get by. We married until God separated us. He was a good father and husband. I breastfed all the children until they were fifteen to eighteen months old and by the time I had my last one I was ashamed to show my breasts.

María Borjas

Rosario had my luck bringing up her children without their father, having to make sacrifices, working, suffering because she was a Sandinista, and they put her in prison. How she suffered. It used to be horrible in those days. Now the situation has begun to change, but it's been a hard life.

Rosario Antunez

Rosario Antunez directs the Estelí Adult Education school and is the Ocotal FSLN representative to the National Assembly.

I believe there are two main reasons why people become revolutionaries. One is when all your needs are answered for so you can look beyond yourself towards those less fortunate. The other reason is when you're brought up in abject poverty. To change this you realise that society has to change too, since your suffering is tied to that of your class. And that's what happened to me.

I was brought up on farms. Father came from Honduras. He'd fought the Honduran dictatorship, and was forced into exile. Although I think of him as an intellectual, when he came to Nicaragua he took what work he could find – as a farm labourer. But it wasn't long before he became the farm manager because he was honest, hard-working. But we were always very poor. I never had more than one dress, I remember; when mother washed it I had to wait naked at home until it was dry. Mother cooked for the seasonal coffee workers. The living conditions were terrible, and when a worker fell ill he'd be fired immediately. It would come as no surprise to hear that the poor man had dropped dead on the road. Of course the boss kept no medicines.

Then, after six years, the landlord sent Father to work on his other farm near Ocotal where I began my primary education. I was older than my classmates but quickly caught up and did well in all my exams – so much so that I won a scholarship to go on to secondary school and study teaching in Esteli. I was there when the National Guard attacked the León students and a national students' strike was called in protest. Students from our college joined in.

Father disapproved of me joining in, and insisted that I return to my classes, but I refused to do as he said. Oddly enough, he was the one who'd put these rebellious ideas into my head with all his talk about justice.

Father did have conservative views where I was concerned, and didn't want me to go and teach in Jalapa, up in the mountains. There was a great need for teachers in the rural areas so I was determined to go, even though I dearly loved and respected my parents.

I had been teaching there a year when I met my husband. I had a girl by him but it wasn't long before we separated. He was so bossy. When I look back on why he was like that, I think it was really a product of the repressive atmosphere we lived in.

When I came back to Ocotal I found another teaching job and became involved in the teachers' union. I remember the textbooks I had to use at school were full of dreadful rubbish, like: 'Thanks to our Mother country, Spain, Nicaraguans now have a language.' I was very concerned that my pupils see beyond this type of distortion so used to ask questions like, 'What did the conquistadors bring but domination, syphilis and poverty?' Well, you can imagine it wasn't long before the headmaster had me in his bad books! At times I used to feel isolated. But everything changed in 1974 after a friend visited me. He told me for the first time that he was a Sandinista. I can still remember our conversation: he asked me if I would join as well, and I said, 'Well, why on earth didn't you ask me before? I'd have joined years ago.'

With that sorted out, he said, 'Then I will arrange for someone else to come and talk with you. It'd be best to make contact tonight after Mass when we leave the church. He'll pick us up there, by the shrine of the Virgin Guadalupe. But don't look for him, just keep talking to me.' And all this happened to plan. The contact followed us back to my home.

When the man entered the living room I was overcome by such emotion. It was as though all my hopes and fears

Rosario Antunes visits one of the adult education classes in Estelí

were coming true: the chance to join the struggle. I felt a total happiness – I imagined it was like falling deeply in love. The man introduced himself as Roberto. He said, 'You must be María.' This was to be my new name, and Roberto was really Carlos Manuel Morales. Today he runs the local government in Estelí.

That night he explained a lot, and he said, 'There are two golden rules that you must never forget: never ask for information, and never repeat to anyone what you've been told.' My contact was to be a man called Octavio, pseudonym Alejandro, who would soon come with a

woman called Ruth who'd work with me. Then he asked if I had friends who might collaborate. Before leaving he looked over the house in great detail.

I felt then that I'd found what I'd been looking for. As a teacher I'd felt so angry and sad to see my pupils arrive at school faint with hunger. Here now was the chance to end the people's humiliation. My fears dissolved; I felt totally committed. I didn't think I might die. Or worse, that my daughter would give her life for the revolution.

Ruth soon arrived. She's a wonderful person. Today we know her as Commander Monica Baltadano[1] and we became very close friends. Our work was to build up the Sandinista Front in the region. My time was divided between the children and work. I became a messenger, recruited trusted friends and found safe houses and transport. We would wake at five to study philosophy, and every night did physical training and checked out the movements of the Guard and State Security spies. I'd talk with market sellers, to people I knew, to tell them they too could collaborate if only they'd forget their fear. Gradually people did begin to join. My nephew and niece's husband and three neighbours joined our cell and slowly the Ocotal network grew.

My home became like a crossroads. I'd be going to the bathroom in the middle of the night and suddenly bump into someone. It'd scare me rigid, but still I couldn't ask who they were.

Then someone very special to me came and stayed. He was very ill after an operation, but I was told that once he'd recovered he would be giving me political and military classes. We began by healing his wounds. I made sure he ate well. I knew the hardships endured by these *compas* in the mountains. He was so thin and tense; when he smoked you could see a nervous twitch in his throat. When the political classes finally started he had quite a time as I was always cracking jokes. There was no telling me off because that's the way I am. This man is Commander Omar Cabezas.[2] I adored these *compañeros*, they were my brothers. Another man came to stay who'd never sit still and was always laughing. He too was nervous, yet brave and intelligent, with an air of authority. We called him Oscar, but today he's Commander Bayardo Arce.[3]

At this time my nephew was doing military training at the Macuelizo Sandinista training camp when an informer revealed its whereabouts to the Guard. They attacked on 27 August, but my nephew escaped. The Guard also discovered another centre in El Sauce. Throughout the region there was dreadful repression, in Matagalpa, Jinotega and Zelaya. It was at its worst in the Nueva

Segovia and Chinandega regions. Peasants were captured and badly tortured, and this caused serious damage to the Sandinista structures. Although the cells were fundamentally strong, the weaker people cracked under this torture, and those informed on were caught.

Monica, Bayardo and my nephew and I met with Pedro Arauz[4] to discuss what to do. It was decided that Bayardo and my nephew should leave the area immediately. I felt bad that I couldn't tell my sister where her son had gone; but in the end I didn't know either, because they didn't manage their getaway. Eight Guards stopped them on the Ocotal Bridge. The driver, a collaborator, was ordered out of the truck. He was so nervous that he took out the ignition keys, so the others couldn't speed off. When they searched them and found Bayardo's pistol, Bayardo grabbed the Guard's rifle and fired, and my nephew and Bayardo escaped. The two of them against eight Guards! But the collaborator was caught, and you can imagine what they did to that poor man.

Soon the Guard picked me up and took me in for interrogation. They really fired the questions about my nephew and the Sandinistas, and my mind worked at a rate of knots. For hours, blindfolded, I somehow kept control of the situation. Eventually they let me go. But a month later I was arrested again and this time interrogated in the Guards' barracks. The colonel gave me hell, but I managed to stay calm and decided to try my luck. 'I've committed no crime, so if you'll excuse me,' I said, and got up and walked out. The man could easily have put a bullet through me, but he let me go. Well, he did get me in the end because I was sentenced to five years' imprisonment. This time my spirit felt broken. I couldn't face leaving my children and parents.

I was put into solitary confinement and after three days the attorney tried bribing me by saying my mother was critically ill in hospital: 'If you tell us where your nephew is you can visit your mother.' But it didn't work. They accused me of believing in communism and I'd say, 'No, I